A Guide to
Small Congregation
Religious Schools

A Guide to
Small Congregation
Religious Schools

Lawrence N. Mahrer

Debi Mahrer Rowe

UAHC Press
New York

LIBRARY OF CONGRESS CATALOGING-IN-PUBLICATION DATA

Mahrer, Lawrence N.
   A guide to small congregation religious schools / Lawrence N.
Mahrer, Debi Mahrer Rowe.
     p. cm.
   ISBN 0–8074–0556–6 (pbk : alk. paper)
   1. Jewish religious education of children—United States. 2. Jewish
religious schools—United States. 3. Reform Judaism—United States.
I. Rowe, Debi Mahrer. II. Title.
BM103.M27 1996
296.6'8—dc20   96-9160
                                                 CIP

This book is printed on acid-free paper
Copyright © 1996 by the UAHC Press
Manufactured in the United States of America
10 9 8 7 6 5 4 3 2 1

This manual is dedicated to

- all the parents who entrusted their children to us

- all the children who entrusted their parents to us

- all the wonderful people in our congregations who worked with us in religious education programs as members of the faculty or the Religious Education Committee

- and all the students, children and adults, who studied with us, became our friends, and, we hope, were infected with our love of Judaism

"Jewish Is Joyous"

I *Hear* and I Forget
I *See* and I Remember
I *Do* and I Understand

anonymous

Contents

Acknowledgments

- Rebecca and Louis Lister were the authors of the 1977 UAHC manual on small congregation religious schools. In the early 1970s, Louis was the president of NATE and Rebecca was the secretary of NATE. Both are credited with establishing the FRE certification for the Reform movement's professional educators. The Listers had significant careers in religious education along the eastern seaboard and in the northeast. Rebecca is still living in southern Florida.

- Rabbi Norman Kahan, director of the UAHC Small Congregations Department, originally proposed that we write a new, updated manual, and he has been a constant source of support and encouragement.

- Seymour Rossel, RJE, director of the Commission on Reform Jewish Education, has provided guidance and inspiration.

- Robin L. Eisenberg, RJE, a past president of NATE, the educational coordinator for the UAHC Southeast Council, and soon-to-be chair of the Commission on Reform Jewish Education, provided many of the programmatic and teacher-training concepts quoted in this manual.

- Shirley Barish is the educational consultant to the UAHC Southwest Council and editor of *V'ahavta*, the Southwest Council magazine for educators, from which many programs and special classroom activities in this manual were derived.

- A number of rabbis, religious school principals, and others involved in the religious education programs of Reform congregations responded to our request for documents and other materials that described the organization and procedures of their congregations' religious schools. Some are mentioned by name, most are not. All are appreciated.

- Ann Kuykendall, devoted secretary of Temple Emanu-El, Dothan, Alabama, provided the original, computer-generated hard copy of this manuscript.

Foreword

It goes without saying that every congregation begins as a small congregation. As congregations grow larger, they look back on their early days as more "intimate" times—times when the members knew one another, and the rabbi knew each and every member—parents, their children, and their extended families and relations. There was only one rabbi, and some people remember the time when the congregation could not afford even a part-time secretary. Everyone had to do everything. Decisions were often made by telephoning a few people for their input because they were the few who would be affected by the decision. Parents were the teachers of the religious school, and some parent-teacher also served as the school administrator. Those were the days.

Or, rather, those *are* the days. Today, more than half the congregations of the Union of American Hebrew Congregations consists of fewer than 250 member families. They are our "small" congregations. Most of them will not grow much larger. Their size is determined by geographic location in small towns and cities and by the departure of their young people to larger cities. Even so, most of these small congregations have a population of young people and require a system of religious education.

In 1977, the UAHC published a manual to help small congregations establish their religious schools. In its time, the manual served as a valuable guide, and it has been in use for many years. However, we have been aware for some time that a new guide was needed. Education has changed. We have learned new techniques. We have entered an era of advanced technology that provides new materials and resources. In addition, today we know more about the needs of small congregations than we did in the past.

Much of this new knowledge comes from the fine work of the UAHC Small Congregations Department. Founded in 1987, the Small Congregations Department has provided a source of networking, a means for smaller congregations to share their needs and concerns. It has also generated a national small congregations conference, where workshops and discussion groups address nearly every aspect of the life of the small congregation. We have learned that small congregations are not all alike, although the paths they follow are similar. We have learned that small congregations must meet modern needs in the same way as do their larger counterparts. We have certainly learned that a new guide for small congregational schools was long overdue.

As a result, the UAHC Department of Education and the UAHC Small Congregations Department commissioned this guide. At first, we decided only to repair and update the former manual, choosing the writing team of

Rabbi Lawrence N. Mahrer and Debi Mahrer Rowe for this undertaking. However, based on their years of experience with small congregations, their participation in the small congregation activities of the UAHC, and their combined knowledge—attained through their respective educations in rabbinics and in education at the Hebrew Union College-Jewish Institute of Religion—they shaped an entirely new and effective guide. Filled with insights and resources, *A Guide to Small Congregation Religious Schools* presents a truly comprehensive plan for religious schools in small congregations and a philosophical conception of the potential of Jewish education in the smaller synagogue. The authors' work was carefully read and amplified by suggestions made by Rabbi Eugene H. Levy, Annette Abramson, Hara Person, Kathy Parnass, and Alice Jaffe.

This new work recognizes some of the principal difficulties facing the small congregational school: the inability to provide the more highly skilled teachers available in larger cities—especially teachers skilled in the teaching of Hebrew; the lack of a full complement of classes for all age groups so that curriculum can be more readily conceived and administered; the need for textbooks and multimedia and computer resources that are more easily available to religious schools with larger budgets; and the absence of trained Jewish educators and administrators that bring a measure of professionalism to Jewish education.

This guide, however, recognizes that the small religious school has some very special strengths. It is a place of warmth and sharing. It is, by its very nature, a place where family education succeeds. It is a place where theoretical "curriculum" very often becomes customized and individualized to a degree impossible in larger congregations. It is a place where parental support is generally a given rather than a desiderata. It is a place where the rabbi or rabbinic intern can shape the entire school enterprise without supplanting the very real influence of the parents and teachers who usually volunteer their help. It is a place where the presence of the school maintains a high profile within the synagogue as a whole. These are the strengths that larger congregations seek to develop, while smaller congregations usually possess them innately.

The creation and maintenance of a successful small religious school depends more on emphasizing the strengths of the small congregation than on overcoming the lack of those resources available to larger congregations. The Reform movement has sought to help the small schools in several important ways: The Women of Reform Judaism provides grants-in-aid for teacher training; the National Association of Temple Educators aids schools through their network of regional representatives; the Department of Education makes available resource kits and special programs; the Transcontinental Music Publishers creates educational musical resources; and the UAHC Press provides specialized educational texts and materials.

The Small Congregations Department has not only aided in distributing and funding the distribution of these materials and programs but has also sought, through their own publications, to augment the resources available.

The spirit of Jewish religious education is the same in the small congregation as it is in the large congregation. Reaching children with the message of Judaism, with the gift of Torah, and the inspiration of the rabbis and prophets is the same in both settings. Transmitting Jewish identity from one generation to the next is accomplished also in very similar ways. Therefore, educators and teachers in larger settings can learn a great deal from perusing this guide, although its primary audience is clearly the small congregation.

It is said that, in the time of the Talmud, Joshua ben Gamala set up elementary schools throughout Israel—in villages large and small—for children from the age of six or seven and upwards. (Jerusalem Talmud, *Ketubot* VIII, ad fin.)

And it is taught:

> Rab Judah has told us in the name of Rab: Verily the name of that man is to be blessed, to wit Joshua ben Gamala, for but for him the Torah would have been forgotten from Israel. (*Baba Batra* 21a)

The message here is clear: Any place, irrespective of size, can be a place of Torah. All of us who have had a hand in this book are proud to offer its riches for this generation and the many generations to come. Parents, teachers, and educators—in cities large and small—can benefit from studying what is contained here. And all who work in providing Jewish education deserve the praise afforded to Rabbi Joshua: But for you, the Torah itself would be forgotten.

SEYMOUR ROSSEL
Director, UAHC Department of Education
Director, Commission on Reform Jewish Education

RABBI NORMAN KAHAN
Director, UAHC Small Congregations Department

Preface

In July 1993, the Union of American Hebrew Congregations provided the following information:

1. There are 851 congregations in the UAHC.

2. Of the 851, 477 (63 percent) are small congregations.

3. Of the 477 small congregations, the majority, 274, are "very small," with 100 families or less.

4. Of these, 111 have rabbis and 163 do not.

5. The combined membership of UAHC small congregations, approximately 48,300 households, constitutes 16 percent of American Reform Jews.

The above statistics provide ample evidence of the need for this manual.

In a letter to her congregation just prior to the opening of school in 1993, Rabbi Patricia Karlin-Neumann included the following, which sets the tone for any congregationally oriented religious education program.

When Israel stood to receive the Torah, the Holy One, blessed be the One, said to them: I am giving you My Torah. Present to Me good guarantors that you will guard it, and I shall give it to you.

They said: Our ancestors are our guarantors.

The Holy One, blessed be the One, said: Your ancestors are not sufficient guarantors. Yet bring Me good guarantors, and I shall give you the Torah.

They said: Master of the universe, our prophets are our guarantors.

The One said to them: The prophets are not sufficient guarantors. Yet bring Me good guarantors, and I shall give you the Torah.

They said: Our children are our guarantors.

And the Holy One, blessed be the One, said: They certainly

are good guarantors. For their sake, I give the Torah to you.

Shir Hashirim Rabbah

There is both power and paradox in this story. It is through our children that we are worthy of Torah; for them to be guarantors, we must teach Torah to them. Our inheritance is through our children, but we must give them the legacy. Some of us, as children, were not given the legacy of Torah. Some of us were not schooled or learned little substantive material or learned only until our early adulthood. How, then, can we make sense of the legacy that we must continue for the next generation? How can we fulfill the commandment so pervasive at Pesach: *Vehigadeta levincha*, "And you shall tell your child"? It is through recognizing that we, too, must be learners. In the traditional community, learning is not the province of the young, but of everyone. So, too, for those of us who have not received enough of a legacy to pass it on.

Introduction

A Philosophy of Jewish Education

All Jewish education points to the same basic objective: to lead Jewish children toward a Jewish future. The religious school curriculum will help the student relate to the concepts of God, covenant, and *mitzvot*; will assist the student in identifying with the historic experience of our people; and will lead the student toward active participation in the local and global Jewish community.

> The most frequent mistake made in Jewish child-rearing is asking the question: "What one thing will make the most difference in my child's Jewish future?" Know from the start that the formula for Jewish identity is a blend of many key experiences and connections. There is no one key...Jewish life is Jewish life... Jewish identity is the kind of thing you solve through proper diet, exercise, a combination of treatments...ultimately, dynamic Jewish life, the kind of Jewish lives that in turn produce their own Jewish children, is nurtured, not bred. It is not a question of finding a single element but of building a life path.
>
> *Exerpted from* 40 Things You Can Do to Save the Jewish People
> *Joel Lurie Grishaver, Alef Design Group. Used by permission.*

The purpose of this manual is to illustrate methods and techniques and offer suggestions that will help the small religious school provide optimum education within the limitations of personnel, facilities, resources, and finances with which it must operate.

General Aims of Jewish Education

The role of Jewish education is to provide students with the fundamental skills, information, and values of our tradition that will enable them to lead a more fulfilling life and to carve out a meaningful place for themselves in the Jewish and world communities.

The success of a religious school experience cannot be measured by any objective standard. Evaluating how well information is absorbed or mastered will tell little about the actual outcome of the overall learning experience. The way students choose to behave while participants in the religious school, as well as in the years beyond, is the truest test of the success of a religious education program.

To achieve the goals of any religious education program, the home and school must work together in partnership. Neither can do the task without the other. While the young student may be the primary learner and the classroom the primary learning environment, parents must be co-learners as well as co-teachers.

Goals of Reform Jewish Education

The UAHC Department of Education has set forth the goals listed below. These guidelines foster the deepening of Jewish experience and knowledge for all Jews in order to strengthen faith in God, love of Torah, and identification with the Jewish people through involvement in the synagogue and participation in Jewish life. We believe that Judaism contains answers to the challenges and questions confronting us daily and that only a knowledgeable Jew can successfully discover these answers.

Linked to these goals, the programs of our religious schools embrace experience and learning activities, encouraging children, young people, and adults to become...

- Jews who affirm their Jewish identity and bind themselves inseparably to their people by word and deed

- Jews who bear witness to the *berit*, the "covenant," between God and the Jewish people through the practice of *mitzvot*, "commandments," as studied in the Torah and the classic Jewish literature it has generated and as interpreted in light of historic development and contemporary liberal thought

- Jews who affirm their historic bond to *Eretz Yisrael*, the "Land of Israel"

- Jews who cherish and study Hebrew, the language of the Jewish people

- Jews who value and practice *tefilah*, "prayer"

- Jews who further the causes of justice, freedom, and peace by pursuing *tzedek*, "righteousness"; *mishpat*, "justice"; and *chesed*, "loving deeds"

- Jews who celebrate Shabbat and the festivals and observe the Jewish ceremonies that mark the significant occasions in their lives

- Jews who esteem their own person and the person of others; their own family and the family of others; their own community and the community of others

- Jews who express kinship with *K'lal Yisrael* by actively seeking the welfare of Jews throughout the world

- Jews who support and participate in the life of the synagogue

It is our recommendation that each congregation study the goals of the UAHC and examine its own goals to create a "mission" statement that best reflects what it wants to accomplish.

The Religious Education Committee must attempt to discover what it desires its school to be, to know, to understand, and to accomplish. Once those ideas have been formulated, approved, and set down in writing, it should then be possible to design a curriculum that will assist the faculty in creating the environment for reaching these goals.

To accomplish the goals put forth by the UAHC, one congregation (Temple Israel, Alameda, California) created the following statement:

Our mission is to enable students who complete our religious school...

- to transfer what they learn at school to their homes and lives

- to have a strong, positive Jewish identity

- to know their heritage and history

- to understand the concepts behind and the celebrations of the Jewish holidays

- to have a basic understanding of Torah and Bible

- to understand and feel a commitment to Jewish ethics

- to be able to participate fully in a Reform Jewish service

After the congregation created its ideal "mission" statement, it then designed a curriculum that it hoped would make the mission statement fulfillable and achievable.

Organizational Structure of the School

What follows is based on the tripartite explanation of the role of the synagogue. The synagogue is:

1. *Bet Tefilah*   a house of prayer
2. *Bet Midrash*   a house of study
3. *Bet Kenesset*   a house of gathering

We will, of course, focus on the second function, the role of the synagogue as a house of study. This is particularly true for smaller communities where the congregation may be the only Jewish institution or "address."

Because education is one of the major activities/functions/expectations of the synagogue, its importance must be reflected in all that the congregation does. Congregational organizational structure must mirror this importance as well.

The Board of Trustees has the primary responsibility for all facets of synagogue management, which should include all aspects of the religious education program. In most cases, the board works through a committee system, and so we recommend the establishment of a Religious Education Committee to oversee all the education programs of the congregation. The chairperson of the committee should be a full voting member of the congregation board, either appointed from those elected to the board or holding a seat on the board by virtue of the committee chairmanship.

All decisions, policies, goals, rules, procedures, activities, and so forth that are part of the normal operation of any religious school are the responsibility of this Religious Education Committee. All these matters should be fully discussed by members of the committee. Once approved, they should be put in writing and submitted to the congregational board for acceptance, thus becoming the policies of the synagogue itself. In this way the religious education program is assured a major role in the workings of the congregation, directly under the control of its elected representatives.

Even in the smallest schools, this committee should consist of at least five people, one of whom would serve as chairperson, appointed by the congregation president. While all these individuals need not be parents of children enrolled in the school, some of them should be. The committee should also reflect the demography of the synagogue membership. For example, if a substantial number of families live in very small communities twenty miles or more away from the synagogue building, one committee member should be drawn from that group, assuring that its members' interests and problems are considered during committee deliberations. One member of the committee might be a parent with a youngster in the preschool or primary grades, and another might be a parent with a child in the junior high, middle school, or high school. It might also be advisable to include a faculty member and/or an older student as a representative of his/her constituency. Again, this is suggested so that the concerns of this member's group are addressed whenever the committee meets.

If the congregation is large enough to employ a full-time rabbi or even a part-time rabbi who lives in the community, that rabbi should be fully responsible for the day-to-day operation of the religious school. This is an additional way in which the congregation can indicate to its members the very high priority it places on educational activities and programs. If the congregation does not have a rabbi, a member of the Religious Education Committee should assume the responsibility of being the school principal for the entire school year. In either case, the following suggestions are relative to the role of this individual:

- The rabbi/principal should be a full member of the Religious Education Committee, making every possible effort to attend each meeting and participate fully.

- The rabbi/principal should be present at every session of the religious school, unless other rabbinical duties make that impossible.

- The rabbi/principal should be visibly present in the building to welcome students and parents personally as they enter for the religious school and visibly present to say goodbye to the children and their parents at the end of the religious school morning.

- The rabbi/principal should visit every classroom for a few minutes whenever the school is in session in order to monitor and thus assist members of the faculty, as well as to answer questions beyond the scope of the classroom teacher. This procedure further illustrates the importance of the entire educational process.

- The rabbi/principal, therefore, should not be expected to teach classes or to have other responsibilities while the religious school is in session.

- The rabbi/principal should be responsible for whatever administrative functions are involved in the weekly operation of the school, such as collecting *tzedakah*, picking up attendance forms, administering discipline, and so forth.

- The rabbi/principal should be responsible for the planning and the conducting of the school assembly, which should be part of each religious school morning.

- The rabbi/principal should be responsible for communications between the school and the home.

- The rabbi/principal, working through the Religious Education Committee, should be responsible for preparing the annual budget of the religious school. This budget must be approved by the committee and then submitted to the Board of Trustees for acceptance and inclusion in the general budget of the synagogue.

- The rabbi/principal should be responsible for the training programs for religious school teachers.

The costs for operating the religious school must be reflected in the overall operating budget of the synagogue. When the Religious Education Committee prepares the budget, it must take into account the following items:

- Faculty salaries

- Textual materials and workbooks

- Teaching supplies, guides, etc.

- Art supplies

- Program supplies

- Teacher-training expenses

- Expenses for possible field trips

- Possible year-end gifts for volunteer teachers

The list above is not all-inclusive. It does not take into account special circumstances in an individual synagogue. However, it is important for the Religious Education Committee to be as accurate as possible in projecting the expenses for the operation of the synagogue's religious education program. After approval by the committee, this budget request should be sent to the Board of Trustees for its acceptance and for inclusion in the next year's operating budget of the congregation. The total expense of operating the religious school must be reflected in that budget for reasons already stated.

In many congregations there are religious school fees and Hebrew school fees calculated on a per-child basis. If this situation exists in your congregation, those revenues should be a line item on the income side of the congregational budget. While these fees should be determined by the committee, they should be submitted to the board for inclusion in the budget. Obviously, this entire budgetary process will have to be repeated every year as the circumstances of the congregation change, as the number of students enrolled in varying grades rises or declines, and as the overall size of the school increases or decreases.

We recommend that fees for religious and Hebrew school enrollment *not* cover the full operational costs of these two schools. It is critical that the congregational budget underwrite some of these costs, for this is the only way the general membership of the congregation, particularly those who are not parents of current religious school students, can be made aware of the fact that religious education is a congregational priority.

We know that in many congregations it has been a longtime practice for the sisterhood to raise the money that operates the religious school. While we applaud the efforts of the sisterhood women who have undertaken this responsibility in many congregations for many years, we urge that this practice be discontinued. We strongly believe that the message conveyed to the membership of the congregation must be that religious education is a congregational function to be supported, in every conceivable way, by the congregation itself, not by one of its auxiliaries. It is amazing how attitudes change when people become aware that the congregation is making a significant investment of time, effort, and dollars in the religious school program. In these days when large numbers of children come from intermarried families and single-parent families, most often headed by a mother, it is important that the religious school be provided with Jewish male role models. Often this is not the case when the school is operated and/or funded by the sisterhood. The goal of the Religious Education Committee should be to involve as many men in as many different ways as possible so they are visible and directly in touch with the children.

Decisions to Be Made

Thirty years ago, Rabbi Lawrence Mahrer assumed a new pulpit. One of his first tasks was to work with the Religious Education Committee to establish the type of religious school described in these pages. That work began in June and was approved by the Board of Trustees in December with the understanding that all aspects of the school would be implemented when school resumed in January after the midwinter break.

The first Sunday of the religious school term in January began with a combined meeting of students and parents. No student was permitted to attend unless accompanied by a parent. All the changes were introduced and explained. In the middle of this process, students were sent to their classrooms where the specifics of their new curriculum were described by their teachers. Following the parent meeting, one father, with a look of intense anger on his face, confronted Rabbi Mahrer with the following words: "You can't do this!" Without relating the entire conversation, we shall simply inform you that this parent objected violently to making Sunday morning another day of "school" for his children. He indicated that if the congregation truly intended to do what had been discussed that morning, he would withdraw his children from the school until such time as the congregation "came to its senses." When asked what he specifically desired, the father responded, "All I need is a place to leave my children for two and a half hours on Sunday morning so I can go sailing."

The incident above is true, and it is extreme. However, a significantly well-organized school will occasionally disturb some parents because of its emphasis on real learning and the transmission of concepts and values, its insistence on compliance with policies and regulations, and its unwillingness to be a Sunday morning "baby-sitting service" for parents desiring to be otherwise occupied. Our good friend Janice Alper, RJE, is fond of saying, "After all, our second name is *school*," and Rabbi David Baylinson has proposed that our Sunday morning program should be called the "School of Religion" because he feels that the emphasis is always on the first word.

Policies, procedures, requirements, and much more will have to be determined to implement any successful congregational religious education program. A variety of such policy/regulations/requirements statements from several congregations will be found in Appendix A. However, at this point, we believe it appropriate to list some of the questions that must be asked about the philosophies and policies that will govern your school.

8

The following list is not all-inclusive. We offer it simply as a guideline:

1. Which children shall be enrolled in the school? Will the school accept only the children of members? Can children of nonmembers also enroll? If they do, are there any special considerations?

2. At what age are children expected to enroll in religious school?

3. If new members of the congregation have children older than the specified enrollment age, how will the school determine into which grade those children will be placed?

4. What type of attendance standards and requirements will be established for the school?

5. What if a child fails to meet that attendance standard?

6. How will the school handle those students who misbehave or are disruptive during school activities?

7. What is the homework policy of the Sunday morning religious school? What is the homework policy of the midweek Hebrew school? How do they differ? Why?

8. Will students be promoted to the following grade automatically when school resumes the following fall? If promotion is not automatic, what factors are to be considered in determining if the student is to be promoted?

9. If a student is not promoted to the next grade, what can be done over the summer months to enable that student to move along with his/her age level in the fall?

10. Is there a requirement for students in some or all grades to attend holiday or Shabbat worship with the congregation? If so, what is the standard, and how will it be enforced?

11. What are the school's hours on Sunday? What are the days and hours for the supplemental midweek Hebrew school?

12. When can parents expect to receive copies of the curriculum and calendar for the school year?

13. Are there any tuition or enrollment fees to be paid? If nonmember families may enroll their children, are their fees different?

14. Are there special fees for supplemental Hebrew studies?

15. In what grade will the consecration ceremony take place? Will it be held on Simchat Torah?

16. At the end of what grade will the confirmation ceremony take place? Will it be held on Shavuot?

17. What instrumentality or methodology will be employed to resolve any difficulties that may arise between a student/family and the school?

The questions above are fairly general and should apply to every aspect of the child-centered religious education activities of the congregation. The questions below are similar, but they are focused specifically on the mid-week or supplemental Hebrew school program of the congregation and include questions relevant to students planning for bar/bat mitzvah.

1. Is there a prerequisite for enrolling in the midweek Hebrew program? Is there Hebrew knowledge that a student must acquire in the Sunday morning religious school before the student can enroll?

2. Is the midweek Hebrew program open to all students or only to the children of members?

3. For how many times per week for how many years does the midweek school meet? What is the duration of each individual class?

4. Is there a specific worship service attendance requirement for those students who are planning for bar/bat mitzvah?

5. Must a student attend the religious school to participate in the Hebrew school program? For how long must a student be enrolled in the religious school to qualify for the midweek Hebrew program? Is it acceptable for a student to begin with the midweek Hebrew program?

6. Can a student be enrolled in the program without expecting to participate in a bar/bat mitzvah ceremony?

7. If that is possible, does the worship attendance requirement apply? What happens if during the last year of the class, the student then decides to have a bar/bat mitzvah ceremony?

8. Is bar/bat mitzvah automatically tied to age thirteen, or must some level of Hebrew knowledge be acquired before the ceremony can be scheduled?

9. Will every bar/bat mitzvah ceremony be conducted according to the usual and standard worship/ritual practices of the congregation, or will families be allowed to change the ceremony to suit their own individual needs or ideas?

10. Is there any parental involvement expected in the bar/bat mitzvah ceremony? How is the situation to be handled if one of the parents is not Jewish?

11. Is there—or should there be—a congregational policy that attempts to regulate the social aspects of the bar/bat mitzvah event?

12. Are there any problems that might be encountered because some students live in surrounding communities that are a considerable distance from the synagogue building?

13. Since differences in academic ability may exist among children within a family, should our bar/bat mitzvah ceremonies be constructed in such a way that these differences are eliminated or minimized?

Below is a third set of questions that relate to preparation for confirmation and the confirmation service:

1. What grade or grades are to be included in the confirmation class?

2. If the congregation has a rabbi, is it the rabbi's responsibility to teach the class? If more than one grade is in the confirmation class, will confirmation be held for only those students who have completed the tenth grade; that is, are students expected to stay in the confirmation class for more than one year?

3. Will children of nonmembers be accepted in the confirmation class?

4. Will the service or confirmation be held on Shavuot? In the evening? In the morning?

5. Will the confirmation class meet at a time separate from regular religious school hours? If not, in those congregations that have a rabbi, what will the rabbi's involvement with two separate programs that meet concurrently be?

6. Will there be a worship service requirement for participation in the confirmation class? Since confirmation involves high school students and many high school activities are held on Friday evenings, how will this possible conflict be handled?

7. Will the confirmation class students be expected to participate in the youth group activities of the synagogue and the regional and national events of NFTY?

8. Will a student have to successfully complete a certain number of years of religious education immediately prior to being admitted to the confirmation class?

9. Will students who observe their bar/bat mitzvah have to continue in the religious school of the congregation through confirmation? Can a student observe bar/bat mitzvah without making such a commitment?

10. What arrangements can be made for those students in outlying communities for whom coming to the confirmation class presents a difficulty?

As indicated previously, the three lists of questions above are not to be considered all-inclusive. They are presented merely as guidelines. We remind you that specific examples of congregational documents based on questions such as those above are found in Appendix A.

To assist your congregation in its discussions relative to bar/bat mitzvah and confirmation, we have included an article from the *Journal of Reform Judaism*, Fall 1987, in which Rabbi Mahrer delineates some of his concepts about the significance and meaning of each of these life-cycle ceremonies. For that article, see Appendix B.

Faculty

The most important element in any religious education program is the classroom teacher. If a classroom teacher is knowledgeable, competent, and creative, that teacher can compensate for deficient textual materials and curriculum emphasis and most other problems that occasionally plague our classrooms. Conversely, a teacher who is not qualified, does not relate well to children, and would rather be doing other things on Sunday morning can make a shambles of even the best texts, curriculum, and students. Therefore, it is our primary responsibility to find faculty members who are committed to Judaism and feel an intense desire to pass on to their students that commitment and their enthusiasm.

Please remember that we are talking about *religious* education. No matter what other qualifications a teacher possesses, if he or she is not actively involved in the affairs of the congregation and the Jewish community, that teacher loses effectiveness. Quality teachers are role models outside their classroom: At worship, at adult education activities, and at other congregational functions they demonstrate their commitment to what they teach. We would suggest that during the religious school assembly on Sunday, those teachers who were present for worship on Shabbat should be publicly commended, and students should be encouraged to give a round of applause to any teacher who enrolls in a congregational adult education program. Students are gratified to know that their teachers are studying and learning just as they are.

How do we go about finding people who fit this description? In reality, such people do exist among our members. Unfortunately, however, teaching religious school is not frequently seen as a high-status responsibility, and because it is not so perceived, many qualified individuals are uninterested in participating in the profession. Possibly, the long-term solution is to change attitudes regarding those who teach our children. The congregation needs to find ways to honor and reward faculty members in public at the beginning of the religious school year, when school resumes after the midwinter break, and at the end of the school year. Congregations find ways to involve lay members in conducting some aspects of the services during the High Holy Days. Why not involve the religious school faculty members in those honors on the morning of Rosh Hashanah or Yom Kippur? Would it be possible to have a Shabbat dinner preceding or following services for the entire religious school community on the second or third weekend in January, at which time teachers would be given a special gift or would be honored in some other significant way? If the congregation concludes its school year with a religious school Shabbat at which time awards are presented to students for attendance, achievement, and so forth, why not honor our teachers by asking them to conduct the service that Friday evening or to conduct the Torah service, including the reading of the Torah and haftarah portions? These are a few possibilities. The more we show our respect, appreciation, and gratitude to our faculty with the entire congregational family present, the better are our chances of convincing people of the important status and prestige of the faculty of the religious school.

Many of our smaller congregations begin faculty recruitment from among the parents of the students in the religious school. We suggest beginning that recruitment from among the following groups:

- Those who attend services on a regular basis

- Those who have successfully completed some of the congregation's adult education courses

- Those who are trained in secular education

In addition, if there is a college or university in the community or nearby, it could be possible to recruit teachers from the student body or the faculty. If the synagogue is located relatively close to a metropolitan area, recruit faculty members by talking to the rabbis and/or professional educators associated with the congregations in that community. In addition, if the community has a Jewish community center, the staff members of that facility could suggest individuals who can teach. In any case, if we find teachers who live outside the community, we should consider financial inducements for them to make the trip. Offering to pay for their mileage expenses on a monthly basis could be sufficient inducement.

Some smaller congregations have solved the problem of teacher recruitment by dividing their religious school year (generally about thirty sessions) into smaller components. Frequently, adults who are unwilling to commit to teaching from September through May might be willing to teach a unit of study for five or six to eight or ten consecutive weeks. This method could also present an opportunity to tap into the special interests and special knowledge of some of the congregation members. For example, an older adult who has lived in the community for his or her lifetime could lead a unit for a middle- or upper-grade class on the history of the local Jewish community and/or the history of Jews in the state. For an upper-grade class, a physician or nurse could lead five or six discussions on bioethics. Individuals in the community with special skills in art, drama, dance, or photography could work with a class or group of classes for a maximum of eight to ten weeks on a project for the entire congregation as a culminating activity. There obviously are such individuals among the membership of our congregations. We need a creative approach to utilizing their talents and abilities.

It would be best if teachers for the fall were lined up in the late spring or early summer so that some teacher-training sessions could be scheduled during July, August, and early September before classes begin. Among the resources available to the congregation for such teacher-training programs could be master teachers from your public school system or from an area private school, professors who teach education courses in a nearby college or university, professional religious educators from a large congregation in a relatively nearby community, and anyone else whose expertise you can co-opt. Of course, if your congregation has a full- or part-time rabbi, that rabbi can lead a few sessions dealing with the Judaic content of your curriculum. In addition, every UAHC region has an educational consultant available. Generally, the consultant is a professional educator on the staff of one of the large congregations in the region. If your small congregation could get together with other large or small congregations in your immediate area, it might be arranged to have that educational consultant conduct a full day of workshops for religious school teachers.

In any teacher-training activities, some very specific areas must be covered as thoroughly as possible:

1. Teachers must be made aware of the goals, objectives, policies, and regulations of the school in which they are to teach.

2. Each teacher must know the specific goals of the curriculum for which he or she is responsible.

3. Teachers must know how their particular courses fit into the total curriculum of the religious school.

4. Teachers should be assisted in lesson planning...

    -   to make sure there are diversified activities in the classroom at each session

    -   to make certain they plan balanced sessions, not too much and not too little

    -   to satisfy the day-to-day goals of the curriculum

    -   to recognize whether or not the students have reached those goals

5. Teachers must know the policies of the congregation relative to discipline and how to handle disruptive students in the classroom.

6. Homework must be an area for discussion to enable teachers to develop skills in creating appropriate and meaningful assignments.

7. Teachers must be sensitized to the makeup of the school's enrollment in order to plan how to incorporate into the curriculum the realities of the students' backgrounds.

8. Teachers must learn to balance diverse, sometimes conflicting, requirements for students, including gifted students and those with special needs.

Expenses for some teacher-training activities should be assumed by the congregation to reflect the priority the school places on its religious education program. Covering teachers' costs automatically may motivate teachers to attend training workshops and help some decide to become faculty members. Other costs of teacher training may include an honorarium for a visiting instructor, travel expenses that enable faculty members to attend an institute or workshop held in another community, and the minimal expense of providing faculty members with a meal or snack during teacher-training sessions. These costs should be figured into the religious school budget and covered by the general operating budget of the congregation.

In their manual for the smaller religious school, originally published by the UAHC in 1977, Rebecca and Louis Lister included a document by Max Rosenberg entitled *The Image of a Good Teacher*. The following is a slightly edited version:

A Good Teacher...

- knows and accepts the objectives of his/her school

- has a good background in and knowledge of Judaism

- has a clear overview of the entire school curriculum

- knows thoroughly the course of study for the grade he/she is going to teach

- possesses the characteristics of enthusiasm, pleasantness, patience, and firmness in healthy combination

- appreciates the uniqueness and potentiality of each child in the class

- understands the psychology of children in the age group he/she teaches

- understands the specific psychological factors in the lives of his/her students, including recent events such as death or divorce

- always seeks to better understand and guide each individual in the class
- knows and adheres to school policies, procedures, and forms
- plans classwork with care and thoroughness
- makes full and proper use of supplemental teaching aids to enrich teaching
- employs continuity, variety, and depth in creating a class of interested, motivated students
- makes the classroom a place of "joy in learning"
- seeks consciously and constantly to improve his/her teaching and himself/herself as a teacher
- keeps informed of and becomes actively involved in synagogue activities
- seeks to make creative contributions to the improvement of the school
- understands that he/she is teaching not academic subject matter but *a way of life*
- appreciates his/her role as an influence in the lives of students
- is dedicated to the task of developing good Jews and fine human beings

Curriculum

Structure and Content

Because this curriculum has been prepared for small congregational schools without enough students for individual classes in each grade, we have developed it as a two-year rotating system. The exception, however, is that the curriculum anticipates a separate kindergarten class each year. Every fall, students who were in kindergarten the previous year will move into the combined first/second grade class. Second graders who were in the combined first/second grade class the previous year will move into the combined third/fourth grade class. This same upward movement continues through all grades, culminating in the two-year confirmation class. Only those students who have completed the tenth grade will participate in the confirmation ceremony. We feel that it is advantageous for individual students in a learning environment to have different classmates every other year.

The curriculum for each grade is often expressed in the form of questions because we feel this format will help the volunteer teacher focus on specific subject matter. Moreover, some of these questions are repeated at different grade levels because students will approach this same material with deeper intellectual understanding and maturity.

In developing this curriculum, we have constantly referred to "Goals of Reform Jewish Education" as described in the introduction to this manual. We believe this curriculum will assist the small religious school in achieving the educational goals set forth by the Reform movement. However, any curriculum created by two people who are unfamiliar with your community may not be able to address the ramifications of specific situations within your congregation. Therefore, the curriculum is intended to serve as a guide that your Religious Education Committee will modify to fit your own special circumstances.

No specific books have been recommended at any grade level, but texts suitable to this curriculum are available from a variety of publishers. In some cases, the publications will be useful for the classroom teacher only; in others, there will be specific textbooks for use by the students. Most publishers have developed a teacher's guide for many of their textbooks. These guides are valuable tools for experienced as well as novice teachers. Some textbooks have been created with separate corollary workbooks; others have included student exercises and activities as part of the textbook. In short, there is a variety of resources for both teachers and Religious Education Committee members to help enhance your school's curriculum. Choose the products that effectively satisfy the needs of your students, your teachers, and the congregation as a whole.

We recommend that the Religious Education Committee begin its search for appropriate textual material by obtaining catalogs from the following major non-Orthodox Jewish educational publishers: the UAHC Press, Behrman House, Ktav, A.R.E., and Torah Aura Productions.

In the "Resources" section of this manual, we have included a much more extensive listing of publishers and purveyors, complete with addresses and phone numbers.

Curriculum Outline

	God	Torah	Israel
Kinder-garten	*Shema, Hamotzi*	Exploration of the Torah	Who are the people in our synagogue community?
1st/2nd Grades	What happens when we pray? Does God hear our prayers?	Stories of people in the Torah Stories of other biblical people	Stories from the backgrounds of our members
3rd/4th Grades	Where have *you* found God? How do you bring God into *your* life?	Close reading of selected biblical texts	An imaginary visit to places in Israel
5th/6th Grades	What happens when we pray? Does God hear our prayers?	Study of the weekly Torah portion Variety of Jewish religious literature	State of Israel: land, country, people Current events relating to Israel and Jews around the world
7th/8th Grades	Where have *you* found God? How do you bring God into *your* life?	Development of biblical literature Nonreligious Jewish short stories	Typical American Jewish community organization, including field trips
Confir-mation Class	What must we do to find God? Overview of Jewish theologies	Torah reading and presentation of *Devar Torah* for the congregation once a year	What unites Jews around the world?

Celebrations	Ethics	Prayer/Ritual	
Shabbat	Introduction of terms: *mitzvah, tzedakah, betzelem Elohim*	Synagogue people and places	**Kinder-garden**
Introduction to holidays: identification of ritual objects Introduction to life cycle: identification of ritual objects and people	Introduction of concepts: *bikkur cholim, gemilut chasadim, pikuach nefesh*	Identification of objects in the sanctuary: *Ner Tamid, Aron Hakodesh, Menorah, Aseret Hadibrot, Sefer Torah*	**1st/2nd Grades**
Holidays; a holiday story and its central theme Life cycle: values inherent in each ritualized moment	Introduction of concepts: *bal tashchit, tza'ar ba'alei chayim, tikkun haolam*	Hebrew reading readiness Learning to read Hebrew	**3rd/4th Grades**
Holidays: appropriate *berachot* and their meaning Life cycle: focus on bar/bat mitzvah	Comprehensive study of previously learned values	Covered in Hebrew school	**5th/6th Grades**
Focus on family celebrations and observances with parents Cooking foods for the various holidays	Living values/ doing values/class projects	Conducting a religious school service Exploration of themes, structure, and personal meaning of liturgy	**7th/8th Grades**
Focus on "choosing" to be Jewish	Social action	Conducting a portion of Shabbat worship for the congregation once a year	**Confir-mation Class**

With regard to Hebrew education, this curriculum is based on three assumptions:

1. Since each child in the school will be expected, at the minimum, to learn to read Hebrew, Hebrew will be taught in the fourth grade.

2. The congregation will provide a supplementary Hebrew school in the fifth, sixth, and seventh grades, which will also prepare students for bar/bat mitzvah.

3. The curriculum will focus on liturgical Hebrew since most adults and children in our communities use Hebrew primarily for worship and ritual in the synagogue and the home. The synagogue and home settings will reinforce each other in this curricular choice.

Grade Level Curricular Notes

In this section, we will expand on those areas of the Curriculum Outline chart that we feel need more of an explanation than space on the chart allowed.

Kindergarten

We have assumed that kindergarten is the entry level for the school. The year's curriculum focuses on introductions to many subject areas and builds a foundation for future studies. At this age level, it is important that students have the opportunity to touch and experience firsthand as much as possible.

God: Students should learn both the *Shema* and *Hamotzi* in class in order to be able to recite them during school assemblies, at snack time, and at home. In addition, opportunities should be provided for children to discuss what these two prayers mean in their lives.

Israel: Throughout the curriculum, the term *Israel* is used for both the Jewish people and the State of Israel. At this level, we look at the people who make up the staff and membership of our most immediate Jewish community, our synagogue.

Celebrations: At all levels throughout the curriculum, the content should embody both theory and practice: "how-to"and "why?" for holidays and life-cycle ceremonies. We begin with Shabbat because of its frequency and importance.

First/Second Grades

God: Students must be encouraged to express freely their own ideas, concepts, and opinions. They do not have to agree with their rabbi, parents, teachers, or friends. Recognizing that our tradition places a high value on a variety of different answers to the same question, we must support students' ideas.

Torah: One year of the curriculum should include stories of the people in the Torah; the other year should deal with stories of people from the other two parts of the Bible: the Prophets and the Writings.

Israel: Individual members of the congregation should be invited into the classroom to share their own personal histories. In this way, the students will be able to explore the wide variety of Jewish backgrounds (geographic, religious, ethnic, educational, etc.) of these people and the communities in which they grew up. The students will also learn why these people came and stayed in your community.

Ethics: Throughout the curriculum, ethical terms and concepts will be presented to the students so that they may attain the following goals: to learn the terms *in Hebrew* to demonstrate Jewish literacy; to explore the concepts that underlie these terms; and, through opportunities provided by the school, to perform the *mitzvot* associated with these concepts. The students need to know that even a child can be *mekayem mitzvah,* a "performer of the *mitzvah.*" A concrete example: Although young children may not be able to visit a hospital room, they can (and should) create cards, record songs, make gifts, etc., to perform the act of *bikkur cholim,* "visiting the sick."

Third/Fourth Grades

Torah: At this age, children are usually accomplished readers. In fact, this is probably their "voracious reading" phase. It is, therefore, appropriate at this time to introduce the students to the classic texts of our tradition. It is important to utilize authentic translations of the texts prepared in an age-appropriate manner. We are not dealing with "Bible stories" but with the biblical text itself in an English rendition suitable for these grades. This approach continues through the sixth grade of this suggested curriculum.

Israel: This is the introduction to the State of Israel. At this basic level, students should "visit" Israel via slides, videos, text material, and reports from those who have visited or were born there. Use as many media as possible.

Prayer/Ritual: The fourth grade will be the only time in the structure of this model religious school when the combined class will be separated. Only the fourth graders will be taught to read Hebrew. The third graders will begin a program of Hebrew reading readiness and will be involved in other classroom activities while the fourth graders are studying Hebrew.

Fifth/Sixth Grades

Torah: Students will be introduced to the actual texts of such postbiblical rabbinic writings as the *Mishnah*, *Gemara*, Midrash, and responsa.

Seventh/Eighth Grades

Torah: Now that students have been introduced to some of our ancient religious texts, it is appropriate for them to discover how events and circumstances effected the development of the texts over time.

In addition, students will read a variety of nonreligious Jewish short stories. A great deal can be learned from the vast world of Jewish fiction. A number of anthologies are available, or the teacher can make a personal selection of stories to be read. It is suggested that each story be approached with these three questions:

1. Why do you think the author wrote this story?

2. What do you think was the message the author attempted to convey?

3. What Jewish things did you learn from this story?

Israel: Our experience has taught us that children in our congregations who grew up in an isolated Jewish community are frequently overwhelmed when they first move into a large, fully organized Jewish community. They are totally unaware of the multitude of Jewish organizations that exist and what these organizations accomplish; they are unfamiliar with the variety of synagogue experiences and styles they encounter, as well as the many Jewish life styles and levels of observance they see about them. It is impossible to learn about these situations exclusively in a classroom setting. Our strong recommendation is that a field trip to a large, well-organized Jewish community be undertaken in each of the two years.

Furthermore, we strongly recommend a TV/VCR setup as essential for the religious school. Through feature movies, recordings of TV episodes, Jewishly produced specialized videos, etc., students can be exposed to many "kinds" of Jews and Jewish communities beyond their own.

Tzedakah

*T*zedakah is a Hebrew word frequently translated as "charity." However, this translation is not adequate to explain the concept. The word derives from the basic Hebrew root *tzedek*, meaning "justice." Thus, *tzedakah* comes closer to meaning just treatment or what is proper or expected. In Jewish tradition, every Jew is required to perform the *mitzvah* of *tzedakah*. Even the beggar is expected to take a small portion of what he receives and donate it to others who are less fortunate.

Tzedakah should be collected in every classroom each week. There are many ways teachers can connect the collection of *tzedakah* with the subject matter being studied or with a particular theme. Teachers should urge parents to remind their children to bring money for this *mitzvah*. It would be best if each family could select specific tasks for children to accomplish at home so the money used for *tzedakah* comes from the child's own effort. The size of a child's weekly contribution is much less important than the concept of giving the donation. It is that concept we wish children to learn.

In some religious schools, each class keeps a record of the *tzedakah* collected. At the end of the school year, the students in that class then determine how the total is to be divided and to whom it is to be donated. In some smaller schools, the entire student body is involved in making those decisions.

However this process is worked out, it is very important that students be knowledgeable about the organization to which they are donating. To bring a quarter or a dollar to religious school at the end of each week and put it into a *tzedakah* box or jar without any knowledge of where that money will go, how it will be used, and how it will benefit others misses the point.

Therefore, in Appendix C, you will find a reprint of an article originally published in *Compass*, the religious education magazine of the UAHC/NATE. The article appeared in the Summer 1984 issue. In fact, that issue contains five major articles on the basic concepts of *tzedakah* and their implementation in our religious education programs. Contact the UAHC to determine if additional copies of that issue of *Compass* are still available.

Maimonides, one of Judaism's most prominent rabbinic authorities, codifiers, and philosophers, lived in Spain and Egypt from 1135 to 1204. He taught that there are eight degrees or steps of *tzedakah*:

- The first and lowest degree is to give, but with reluctance or regret. This is the gift of the hand, but not of the heart.

- The second is to give cheerfully, but not proportionately to the distress of the sufferer.

- The third is to give cheerfully and proportionately, but not until solicited.

- The fourth is to give cheerfully, proportionately, and even unsolicited; but to put it in the poor man's hand, thereby exciting in him the painful emotion of shame.

- The fifth is to give charity in such a way that the distressed may receive the bounty and know their benefactor, without their being known to him. Such was the conduct of some of our ancestors, who used to tie up money in the corners of their cloaks so that the poor might take it unperceived.

- The sixth, which rises still higher, is to know the objects of our bounty, but remain unknown to them. Such was the conduct of those of our ancestors, who used to convey their charitable gifts into poor people's dwellings, taking care that their own persons and names should remain unknown.

- The seventh is still more meritorious; namely, to bestow charity in such a way that the benefactor may not know the relieved persons, nor they the name of their benefactors, as was done by our charitable forefathers during the existence of the Temple. For there was in that holy building a place called the Chamber of the Silent, wherein the good deposited secretly whatever their generous hearts suggested, and from which the poor were maintained with equal secrecy.

- Lastly, the eighth, and the most meritorious of all, is to anticipate charity by preventing poverty; namely, to assist the reduced fellow-man, either by a considerable gift, or a loan of money, or by teaching him a trade, or by putting him in the way of business so that he may earn an honest livelihood and not be forced to the dreadful alternative of holding out his hand for charity. To this Scripture alludes when it says: And if thy brother be waxen poor, and fallen in decay with thee, then thou shalt relieve him; yea, though he be a stranger or a sojourner; that he may live with thee. This is the highest step and the summit of charity's golden ladder.

Reprinted from the *Union Prayer Book*, vol. II, CCAR, 1945, pp. 117-118

This series of statements about *tzedakah* should be included for discussion in every religious school classroom every year. As students grow older, more capable of deeper understanding, and more mature, they will approach these ideas on a different and deeper level. An understanding of these teachings of Maimonides will help students realize that *tzedakah* is not merely the donation of money at each religious school session.

Moreover, *tzedakah* does not have to be limited to a weekly collection of money. The very best *tzedakah* program involves the students in hands-on experiences that creative religious educators can often implement. For example, just prior to the Purim holiday, students could prepare and distribute *Shalach Manot* to a family in the congregation with with a new infant or to members of the congregation who are homebound or aged. The *Shalach Manot* baskets may be prepared for these families or individuals and delivered to them on the Sunday morning immediately prior to Purim. Of course, these individuals and/or families should be asked in advance if they are willing to have religious school students visit them, and a specific date and time should be established.

The entire religious school can "adopt" a poor family with children who are in the same age group as the students. Information about such a family can be obtained from the principal of a school in a low-income area of the community or from one of the social welfare agencies in town. Once a family has been selected, the students can determine the best way to help that family:

1. The religious school students can conduct a food drive two or three Sundays prior to Thanksgiving and deliver the food on the Monday or Tuesday immediately before the holiday.

2. The students can purchase individuals gifts for the children in the family. Obviously, it will be necessary to know the children's ages if toys are to be given and their sizes if clothing is to be given.

3. The students may decide to give a gift to the children in the family on their birthday.

Whatever means is chosen by the individual religious school, the students should become involved directly in the lives of others in their community who would benefit from their assistance. We can help our students develop habits through a variety of experiences that create attitudes. Student experiences involving kindness and the performance of *mitzvot* generally are more effective and longer lasting than time spent in classroom discussion.

In their 1977 manual, the Listers included the following comments in their discussion of *tzedakah*: "The Keren Ami program should primarily be an educational program and only secondarily a fund-raising campaign." In addition, they wrote, "Let us do acts of *tzedakah*—not merely read about it!"

Assemblies / Worship Services

The religious school day should include an assembly. In our congregations, we frequently talk about "family" and/or "community." An assembly offers a wonderful opportunity to demonstrate this concept.

The assembly should consist of at least some of the following elements:

1. A worship service appropriate for the age group

2. Announcements of future events/activities even though publicity material is sent home with the children or through the mail

3. A discussion of the *tzedakah* program: how much has already been collected, to whom it will be given, and what the organization does with the funds

4. Recreational singing

5. Singing practice of liturgical materials or songs needed for future holiday celebrations

6. Special presentations by invited guests

7. A special performance—song, dance, drama—prepared by a class as part of its curricular work

Consider scheduling the assembly during the religious school morning. If the presence of parents is desired, the assembly should be planned as the first or last activity. This will be more productive than having parents attend in the middle of the school morning. However, if the assembly is intended to provide a break between classroom activities, the middle of the morning will be best.

For the worship component of the assembly, we suggest that it follow as closely as possible the regular liturgical pattern of the congregation and should be both a worship and an educational experience. The children should automatically become familiar with the congregation's mode of worship, melodies, and so forth. If there is a congregational rabbi, that person, whenever possible, should conduct the worship portion of the assembly. However, our curriculum suggests that the students conduct an occasional assembly service.

Library

It is assumed that every congregation has at least a small library. That library can and should be an essential aspect of the religious education program.

Part of the responsibility of the Religious Education Committee should be to advocate and petition for the growth of the library. Through a national or regional company, the committee could conduct an annual book fair, with the profits designated for the acquisition of new materials, either books or videos. Congregants should be encouraged to donate to a library fund (if one does not exist, the board should be encouraged to create one) for *simchas* and as memorials. Rabbi Lawrence Mahrer has been very successful in soliciting books and videos for the synagogue library from congregants. Such a campaign can be conducted every two or three years. Many of our major Jewish publishers have programs through which synagogues automatically receive one copy each of their publications, frequently at a substantial discount. If the congregational budget can absorb the cost, we recommend enrolling your school in one or more of these programs. The following are some programs of this type: the UAHC EMeS program, the Behrman House GOLEM program, and the Torah Aura Productions Club Ed.

The religious school library can be used in a number of ways:

1. Classroom visits designed for students to select books for recreational reading. This can be done effectively three or four times during the school year. To make certain that previously borrowed books are returned before new ones are checked out, the classroom teacher should keep a list of those books borrowed, in addition to the normal library checkout process.

2. Individual use for research on an aspect of the class curriculum. While most students are familiar with this use of the library from their secular education experience, this procedure needs to be demonstrated in the religious education setting so children will learn about some of the major Jewish reference materials, especially some of the Jewish encyclopedias. The students will also become aware of some of the more scholarly English texts that deal with aspects of Jewish heritage/history/tradition. In addition, textbooks other than the one currently being used in their classroom can be successfully utilized for student research.

Should We Operate Our Own School?

We have saved this very important question until congregations have read this manual and obtained whatever guidance we could give about running a small congregation religious school.

After the manual has been read, discussed, and digested, we feel it would then be appropriate for the congregation to answer the question in the title of this section. It is one of the most fundamental questions for a congregation. In the section titled "Organizational Structure of the School," we discussed the three aspects of the role of the synagogue and indicated that the synagogue as *bet midrash*, a "house of study," is one of its most important functions. How then can a congregation be asked if it should operate its own religious school? There are circumstances where the school population is so small that the congregation would surely reply to the question in the negative. However, there are some alternative solutions to this problem that will be discussed below.

Three options come to mind:

1. Enrolling your students in a larger religious school of a nearby congregation

2. Merging your religious school with that of another small congregation in the same community

3. Merging your religious school with another small congregation school in a nearby community

All these options have been utilized by Reform congregations with great success. Because many small congregations are located in towns removed from metropolitan communities, member families who live in these outlying areas must drive up to an hour each way to bring their children to religious school on the weekend and to Hebrew school during the week. The three alternatives listed above are based on the assumption that these families are willing to commit themselves and their time to assure a quality religious education for their children.

We cite the example of a small congregation that has a full-time rabbi and a membership of approximately fifty families but fewer than ten children of religious school age. For a number of years, this congregation successfully operated its own religious education program, but as the number of available children continued to dwindle, an alternative was sought. This synagogue is located approximately twenty-five miles from a much larger city, where there is a Reform congregation with a membership of approximately two hundred and eighty families. Arrangements were made for the students from the smaller congregation to attend religious school in the larger community. Although the bylaws of the larger congregation limited religious education to members, by special action of the board, that requirement was waived for this special set of circumstances. Members of the smaller community enrolled their children in the religious school of the larger congregation, paying only the standard registration fee and any other extra costs that were required of all families with children in the school. This arrangement has continued for the last five to seven years and will continue into the foreseeable future as the median age of the members of the smaller community continues to increase substantially.

In regard to the second option, it has recently been brought to our attention that in the UAHC Southeast Council, headquartered in Miami, a significant number of congregations have merged their religious schools with those of Conservative congregations in their community. The religious schools were merged because both synagogues were small and were struggling to maintain individual religious education programs. The merger of the religious schools into one school, large enough to be educationally viable, was an instantaneous solution to the difficulties faced by both congregations. However, it took many years of conversation and negotiations to overcome the natural hesitancy of each congregation to give up its individual school. In addition, because the congregations adhered to different movements in American Judaism, the congregants from both movements feared that their individual identity would be lost and their children would be taught views with which they disagreed. These concerns required that the process of arranging the merger be handled carefully. In many such instances, the combined school meets in the building of one congregation for half the year and in the other building for the other half. This arrangement allows each congregation to maintain its individuality and identity while the students experience a true sense of "community" throughout their religious education program. Such mergers have to be approached with the clear understanding that no attempt is being made to merge the congregations themselves and that the merger of the schools is not to be considered a first step in the creation of one congregation for the community. We have been assured that the office of the UAHC Southeast Council will direct any inquiries to the communities where such a merger has taken place. We assume that other UAHC regions will do the same.

The third alternative listed above is the merger of a small religious school with a similar small school in a nearby city. We believe that the most successful example of a merger of this kind is the one that occurred between a Reform congregation in Kenosha and a Conservative congregation in Racine, Wisconsin. Rabbi Dena A. Feingold of Beth Hillel Temple in Kenosha has provided us with considerable documentation of the procedure that was followed and the specific details of the schools that merged. See Appendix D.

Be sure you are cautious in initiating this process for your congregation. First, as we have indicated above, approach the merger of two religious schools as a goal in itself, not as a first step toward the merger of the congregations. These are entirely separate matters, each with significant problems and concerns of its own. Keep the issues as simple as possible to avoid confusion. If there is an interest in merging the congregations, that should be a separate matter, possibly some years down the road, based on the success of the operation of a combined religious school.

In any attempt to merge schools, the most important word is *confidentiality*. If the anticipated merger is discussed in the community before any agreements have been reached, the entire project will probably be destroyed at its onset. The greatest dangers are misinformation and unfounded rumor. Everyone involved in the attempted merger of the religious schools should be supportive of the general concept from the very beginning. While there may be some disagreement about specifics and details, the congregational committees must be committed to the concept of merger. Individuals opposed to the concept will do everything in their power to make the merger impossible. They will be adamant at meetings, talk about this matter to others when they should keep it confidential, and spread misinformation to prevent the merger from ever becoming a reality.

The process should begin with a very *general* discussion by the members of the Religious Education Committee. The purpose of this discussion is to explore only the possibility of the merger, not the specifics or details. If the committee agrees that the possibility exists, it must then agree to some other matters. Above all, *confidentiality* must be the rule. Members of the committee must understand that the issue cannot be discussed with anyone outside the committee meetings. The biggest threats to success are rumor and misinformation.

Once the committee has decided that the possibility of merged religious schools exists, it should then approach the Board of Trustees with the concept. Again, confidentiality must be emphasized, and members of the board must be requested to refrain from discussing the issue with anyone outside the meeting room. Such discussions, which often lead to rumors, will destroy the process before it has an opportunity to succeed.

If the Board of Trustees agrees that exploration of this matter is worthwhile, the Religious Education Committee should create a subcommittee of two or three people who are willing to carry on direct negotiations with the other congregation. It is very important that the members of this subcommittee be chosen only from among those who enthusiastically support the potential merger. Someone from the subcommittee should then approach an individual in a responsible position in the religious education program of the other congregation in the community: "In absolute confidentiality, I want to inform you that, in a generalized way, our congregation would like to explore the possibility of merging our two religious schools. Would you explore this possibility with the members of your congregation responsible for your religious education program? If they agree to a discussion of such a possibility, would you select a small committee of two or three people to meet with us for a discussion of the specific details?"

Understand that there will be some significant obstacles in the way of such a merger:

1. Concepts of territoriality

2. Differences in approaches to Judaism and therefore, to what students will be taught

3. Differences in behavior inside the synagogue buildings

4. Different definitions of Who is a Jew? and, therefore, Who can be educated in your school?

5. Many obstacles that we cannot conceive in advance

A suggested approach is to make two lists, one containing the potential advantages of such a merger and the other the potential obstacles to success. With these two lists constantly in front of the committee members, discussion can be more focused and productive.

If a combined committee representing the two congregations arrives at a negotiated agreement, that agreement should then be taken to the appropriate committee in each congregation for discussion and comment. Following such discussions, the combined committee should again meet to determine if any of the comments should be incorporated into the tentative agreement. The next step in the process is to have the combined committee recommend to the appropriate committee in each congregation that this tentative agreement be recommended to the Boards of Trustees for approval. At this time, the boards should be asked only for an agreement in principle, not for acceptance of the document. If the agreement in principle by the boards has been reached, a meeting should be convened of all parents of students in the religious schools, as well as the parents of young potential students. This is the first time any information of the merger should be made available to the general membership of the congregations.

With the groundwork completed in written form, rumor and misinformation are greatly diminished threats. The purpose of this meeting is to explain the concept and details to those present. To facilitate understanding, copies of the tentative agreement should be distributed to those in attendance. Those present should be invited, even urged, to make comments, suggestions, and criticisms, which should be carefully noted and written down. Following the meeting, the Religious Education Committee should study the parental suggestions and, if appropriate, include them in the tentative agreement. It is then time for the combined committee of both congregations to meet again to formalize the agreement based on input from each Board of Trustees and from the parents involved in the education process in each congregation. This formal agreement should now move through the approval process from the combined committee to the individual Religious Education Committees and, finally, to the Boards of Trustees. Once approved by both boards, the agreement becomes the foundation for the merged schools and the outline for the implementation of the merger.

Parents as Partners

In the introduction to this manual, we emphasized that the success of religious education depends largely on a working partnership between the school and the parents. Without that important link, religious education is meaningless. How can this partnership best be actualized?

The rabbi/educator and the teachers must encourage the development of this partnership. Through an early mailing of the minutes of the initial parent meetings, families can learn how to be good partners in the education process. Emphasize that religious education is a family endeavor.

At the most basic level, parents demonstrate the importance of Jewish education to their family life by driving their children to religious school. The value of Jewish education can be easily eroded by parents who allow other events and activities to interrupt religious school sessions. Parents should plan carefully to ensure that Sunday mornings (assuming that is when religious school meets) are always available. Furthermore, a parent should always accompany a child *into* the synagogue building prior to the start of religious school and should wait *in* the building for the child when classes end. It is vitally important for religious school students to see their parents inside the synagogue building. If they do not, they will believe that religious school and the synagogue are only for young people and the synagogue is unimportant to their parents.

Parents must be kept informed about what goes on in religious school. When a holiday is approaching, the rabbi/educator or the teachers can send home information about the holiday and suggestions for family discussions. Parents should be encouraged to ask what the child can do at home for the upcoming celebration. When asked to participate in a class project, enthusiastic and involved parents set a good example, making the child realize that the teachings of the religious school are valuable.

Parents who show an ongoing and enthusiastic interest in the programs of the school and the day-to-day workings in the classroom demonstrate that they truly value the school and its programs. On a deeper level, parents prove their commitment to education by responding to invitations to participate in school programs. By observing their parents engaged in study and activities, children witness the highest level of commitment to lifelong learning.

Family Education

In Jewish life, study has always been a community process. The ideal is for people (parents and children in this case) to study together and learn from one another. This method stimulates individual growth as both parents and children contribute to the group process. Each person who studies Jewishly is both student and teacher at the same time—learning from others and sharing personal insights with them.

Family education is one of the most rapidly growing areas of Jewish education. There are endless numbers of creative ways to involve families in active learning together. The rabbi/educator should seriously consider incorporating some family education into the religious school curriculum. Children will take what they do in religious school more seriously if they see their parents trying to learn and grapple with Jewish material. Family education also provides a showcase for parents to demonstrate their commitment to their children's Jewish education. Especially for parents who have had little or no Jewish education themselves, this is a wonderful way to begin to open doors to Jewish learning and increase accessibility to Judaism.

The following is a list of some ways to incorporate family education into the religious school year:

1. Designate one class during the year for parents to attend with their children in order to introduce parents to the curriculum.

2. Reserve several days throughout the year (perhaps once a month or every six weeks) for joint learning sessions, giving parents and children the opportunity to share in the exploration of curricular topics.

3. Offer family workshops throughout the year on such specific themes as an upcoming holiday, the prayer book, or the Jewish life cycle.

4. Hold an all-day Shabbaton once a year on a particular theme. The Shabbaton could include some parallel programs for adults and children; some joint programs; and opportunities for group worship, study, and fun.

It is crucial for parents to understand the importance of participating in these programs. The rabbi/educator and the teachers must make it clear that attendance at these programs is expected as part of the child's enrollment in the religious school. To that end, it is helpful to enlist the assistance of several parents to work on planning these programs, especially the more extensive events.

Who Are Jewish Parents? What Is a Jewish Family?

In a discussion of the importance of involving parents in religious education, we must first examine the makeup of Jewish families today. A large number of the families a rabbi/educator is likely to encounter will not be comprised of the stereotypical Jewish mother and Jewish father combination. It is crucial for the rabbi/educator to know the makeup of the student enrollment. This information can be obtained through appropriate intake forms and interviews. It is also important for the rabbi/educator to be sensitive to the particularities of that makeup and to help the teachers be sensitive as well. At some point, it is necessary to make certain that the goals of the parents and the goals of the school do not conflict. A discussion of these issues should be included in the initial teacher-orientation meeting or first-teacher training session.

Intermarried Families

Today, in many families that are seeking a Jewish education for their children, there is one non-Jewish parent. In some families one parent may not have been born Jewish but may have converted. Some families may consider their children Jewish through patrilineal descent. In all these cases, the children will probably have close non-Jewish relatives. Intermarried families and families in which there has been a conversion present unique challenges and needs different from a family in which both parents were born Jewish. Some children in an intermarried family do not even see themselves as Jews. Teachers should replace the basic assumptions they tend to make about religious school students with an approach rooted in the reality of the students' lives.

Teachers must respond sensitively and appropriately to children and their parents in intermarried families. The UAHC Department of Outreach has developed a great deal of material on the subject of intermarried families and conducts teachers' workshops in a variety of UAHC and CAJE settings. The following guidelines for the religious school classroom were created originally for a teachers' workshop:

Teachers in the religious school should...

- understand, respect, and teach Reform Judaism, not comparative religion
- include acknowledgment of patrilineal descent

- clarify for the children what is Jewish and what is not

- respect choices made by parents. If a child seems troubled by competing religious demands, bring the situation to the attention of the rabbi/educator.

- include parents in the learning process whenever possible. Send home explanations of lessons on Jewish symbols, rituals, and holiday observance. Would the lesson be understood by a parent who did not grow up as a Jewish child? Include transliterations of the blessings.

- find out about your temple's Outreach program and the resources available to you from the UAHC and your Outreach coordinator

The Reform Jewish classroom must be a place where children from interfaith families can...

- feel safe asking questions

- experiment and not be rebuffed

- find support for their place in the Jewish community

- feel good about themselves and their family

The Nontraditional Jewish Family

The rabbi/educator also needs to be aware of and sensitive to the reality of the different definitions of today's Jewish family. A Jewish family might be a single-parent family, a family in which the parents are divorced, a family in which there is a stepparent and/or half siblings or stepsiblings, or a family in which the parents are two mothers or two fathers. The spectrum of the appearance of Jewish families is also widening as families adopt African-American children or children from Korea, China, and South America.

As in the case of intermarried families, the inclusion of these differing family configurations requires great sensitivity on the part of the rabbi/educator, the teachers, and the school committee. Much of the success of the student's school experience depends on attention to seemingly trivial but important details. For example, the registration form should allow for possibilities beyond "father" and "mother." Mail should always be addressed correctly, and care should be taken to respect the wishes of the parents. It may be wholly appropriate for a noncustodial parent to receive school mailings, or it may be absolutely inappropriate. A family consisting of two mothers should have the names of both listed on official school lists. Attention to such details shows the family that the religious school and the synagogue welcome them.

Teachers must be made aware of any special circumstances and should receive guidance from the rabbi/educator regarding sensitivity within the classroom. No student should ever be made to feel "different" from the rest of the class. The teacher should allow for a range of possibilities whenever discussing such items as celebrating Passover, designing *ketubot* for an art project, or learning the Hebrew words for family members.

Resources

The following list includes publishers and purveyors of religious educational materials. We recommend that the religious school contact these sources, asking for their catalog and requesting that the religious school be put on their mailing list.

ADL
823 United Nations Plaza
New York, NY 10017
800-343-5540

Alef Design Group
4423 Fruitland Avenue
Los Angeles, CA 90058
800-845-0662

**Alternatives in Religious
  Education**
3945 South Oneida Street
Denver, CO 80237
800-346-7779

Behrman House
235 Watchung Avenue
West Orange, NJ 07052
800-221-2755

BJE of Greater Boston
333 Nahanton Street
Newton, MA 02159
617-965-7350

Constructive Playthings
1227 East 119th Street
Grandview, MO 64030
816-761-5900

EKS Publishing Co.
5346 College Avenue
Oakland, CA 94618
510-653-5183

Enjoy-A-Book Club
555 Chestnut Street
Cedarhurst, NY 11516
516-569-0324

Hadassah
50 West 58th Street
New York, NY 10019
212-355-7900

Jewish Lights Publishing
P.O. Box 237
Sunset Farm OFCS, Route 4
Woodstock, VT 05091
802-457-4000

JNF Dept. of Education
78 Randall Avenue
Rockville Centre, NY 11570
516-561-9100

Jewish Publication Society
1930 Chestnut Street
Philadelphia, PA 19103
215-564-5925

Kar-Ben Copies
6800 Tilderwood Lane
Rockville, MD 20852
800-4-KAR-BEN

Ktav Publishing
900 Jefferson Street
Hoboken, NJ 07030
201-963-9524

Learning Plant
P.O. Box 17233
West Palm Beach, FL 33416
407-686-9456

Reading Ruach
P.O. Box 411302
St. Louis, MO 63141
314-469-7362

Shofar Magazine
43 North Cote Drive
Melville, NY 11747
516-643-4598

Social Studies School Services
P.O. Box 802
Culver City, CA 90232
800-421-4246

SoundsWrite
6685 Norman Lane
San Diego, CA 92120
800-9-SOUND-9

Tara Publications
29 Derby Avenue
Cedarhurst, NY 11516
516-295-2290

Torah Aura Productions
4423 Fruitland Avenue
Los Angeles, CA 90058
800-BE-TORAH

Transcontinental Music
  Publications
838 Fifth Avenue
New York, NY 10021
212-650-4101

Tree of Life Book Club/Book Fair
P.O. Box 115
Boston, MA 02258
617-558-2700

UAHC Press
838 Fifth Avenue
New York, NY 10021
212-650-4121

World Zionist Organization
110 East 59th Street
New York, NY 10022
212-339-6080

APPENDIXES

APPENDIX A

RULES, REGULATIONS, POLICIES, AND REQUIREMENTS

Rules, Regulations, and Policies

Students in the religious school of Beth Israel Congregation are entitled to a wholesome classroom atmosphere conducive to effective learning. It is the responsibility of the Religious School Committee to establish such learning conditions by providing appropriate teachers under adequate supervision. It is the responsibility of the parents to cooperate with the school and encourage their children to be cooperative so that together we can achieve successful Jewish education for the coming generation. To maintain the most effective classroom learning conditions, the following procedures are set forth:

1. Registration in our school shall be limited to children of member families.

2. All children are to enter religious school at the time they enter public school kindergarten, and no children are eligible to enroll prior to beginning public school kindergarten (unless a specific preschool class is organized).

3. New students may qualify for placement into their age grade if their previous religious school education meets the standards and requirements established by our Religious School Committee. Students who do not meet these standards will receive special remedial instruction under the direction of the committee and/or the rabbi.

4. Students are required to attend class regularly. Parents of a

47

child who will be absent should notify the teacher in advance. Students are required to make up work missed through absenteeism and should contact the teacher for the assignment for the next session.

5. Promotion is not automatic. It shall depend upon the student's progress at the end of the year. Attendance, reading homework, written homework, classroom work, test results, and attitude all play a part in determining the progress of the student. Promotion can be denied when, in the judgment of the teacher and rabbi, the student does not meet minimum standards. Should this be a problem, parents will be kept informed throughout the school year.

6. If a student is denied promotion because of excessive absences or for academic or other reasons, the student shall have the opportunity to remedy the situation prior to the beginning of the next school year through independent study or tutoring under the direction of a teacher, the committee and/or the rabbi.

7. The privilege of attending religious school is dependent upon the maintenance of proper conduct by the student. Continued disciplinary problems shall necessitate a conference with the student, parents, and the rabbi. The Religious School Committee may deny the privilege of continued attendance on grounds of misconduct until such time as the committee, the rabbi, and the parents agree that the student is ready to be readmitted to the school. Should attendance be suspended as per the above, it is understood that participation in preparation for bar/bat mitzvah and confirmation shall likewise stop.

8. Attendance at the synagogue worship service for students in the sixth grade and up is considered to be part of the educational requirement. Failure to attend is assumed to be an indication of lack of interest in bar/bat mitzvah and confirmation. (Attendance requirements for those students contemplating participation in these ceremonies are listed under those specific headings.)

9. Religious school sessions begin at 10:00 A.M. and last until noon. Students are expected to arrive prior to the opening of class and to remain until dismissal. Sessions will be held in accordance with the religious school calendar issued to all parents prior to the first session of our school in the fall.

10. The ceremony of consecration will be held for those students in the first grade on the holiday of Simchat Torah.

11. The confirmation ceremony will be held on the holiday of Shavuot for those students completing the tenth grade of religious school.

12. Any problems that arise in the operation of our religious school will be handled by the rabbi. Parents who have questions about the functioning of the school are encouraged to bring those questions to the attention of the rabbi and/or the committee.

Midweek Hebrew School and Bar/Bat Mitzvah Requirements

The Religious School Committee feels that additional, intensive Hebrew study, beyond that offered as part of the regular Sunday morning religious school curriculum, is an important positive factor in a child's Jewish education. Therefore, we encourage participation in the following voluntary program. Attendance is *not* limited to those students who are planning a bar/bat mitzvah. Bar/bat mitzvah is an honor that the congregation extends only to those students who will engage in additional Hebrew studies and will meet other requirements in preparation for the ceremony.

1. The midweek Hebrew school will meet twice per week, beginning in the fifth grade, and will last for three years.

2. To be admitted to the program, the student must demonstrate a reading knowledge of Hebrew.

3. Bar/bat mitzvah candidates in the program are to attend Sabbath or holiday services twice per month during the school year for the last two years of the program (grades six and seven). Bar/bat mitzvah is not a substitute for confirmation. All students in the program are expected to continue religious education through confirmation.

4. It is understood that the ceremony of bar/bat mitzvah will be conducted in accordance with the practices of Reform Judaism and Beth Israel Congregation as interpreted by the rabbi and the proper congregational authorities.

5. The parents of the child involved will be encouraged to be active participants in the ceremony.

6. At the time the student adequately demonstrates preparedness to the rabbi, the rabbi will recommend to the Religious School Committee that the ceremony be scheduled.

7. The rabbi and the Religious School Committee feel that the bar/bat mitzvah ceremony should be a highly significant religious and educational experience for the child and the family and, therefore, parents should make plans for social activities in keeping with the purposes and dignity of the occasion.

It is understood that this midweek Hebrew school and its program of bar/bat mitzvah preparation may present our out-of-town members with some difficulties. Therefore, the rabbi and the Religious School Committee should meet with these parents to establish a personal program that will meet the individual needs of the particular situation and will, at the same time, safeguard the educational integrity of the Hebrew study effort outlined above.

Confirmation Requirements

Early Reform Judaism created the ceremony of confirmation for the more mature middle teen years to provide the youngster with an opportunity to "confirm" his/her faith as a Jew and to assume a rightful role in the Jewish community. Just as the Jewish people at Sinai spoke their acceptance of Judaism as they understood it through that experience and just as each generation that followed also took its place in the tradition as it developed, so our children are called upon to come before their God, their families, their rabbi, and their congregation to say: "Based upon what I understand Judaism to be and upon what it means to me, I am willing to take my place today among all the countless generations that have gone before me. I am willing to declare my acceptance, my confirmation of my Judaism."

In an attempt to reach that level of understanding, the following specific program of confirmation is established:

1. The confirmation program will encompass grades nine and ten of the religious school.

2. The ceremony of confirmation will take place at the end of the tenth grade on the holiday of Shavuot.

3. The candidate for confirmation must successfully complete the curriculum of the religious school and must have been enrolled in a religious education program for the three years immediately prior to entering the confirmation year.

4. Students in the confirmation program will be taught by the rabbi, separate from the regular religious school.

5. Students in the program are required to attend Sabbath or holiday services twice per month during the school year. TYG events, which include worship experiences, will count as one service per weekend.

6. Students in the program are urged to participate in the youth activities of the congregation that will be carried out in conjunction with SEFTY and NFTY of the UAHC. Parents are requested to cooperate in this expectation.

The statement at the conclusion of the material related to the midweek Hebrew school should apply to the confirmation program as well.

Religious Education Policies

Congregation Tifereth Jacob

Bar/Bat Mitzvah

As part of the educational program of the religious school of CTJ, the honor of celebrating bar/bat mitzvah is offered to those students who qualify. It is traditional for the ceremony to take place soon after the young person's thirteenth birthday, but it may be held anytime thereafter.

The following requirements have been established by the Board of Directors, the rabbi, the Ritual Committee, and the School Board:

- The candidate for the bar/bat mitzvah ceremony must be of the Jewish faith.

- The family must be a member of this synagogue for at least two years prior to the ceremony.

- The child must have attended and satisfactorily completed the prescribed courses in the religious school at CTJ or an equivalent Jewish institution for at least four years immediately preceding the ceremony. Exceptions will be considered on an individual basis by the rabbi and the School Board, providing the academic requirements are not compromised.

- The child is expected to attend the religious school during the *entire* academic year of the bar or bat mitzvah ceremony, in accordance with the religious school attendance requirements delineated below.

- Both parents and students are required to attend a minimum of twelve Friday night Shabbat services during the year preceding the ceremony and at least eight Saturday morning Shabbat services, especially during the months immediately preceding the bar/bat mitzvah date.

Attendance

Students in the religious school must be in attendance 75 percent of the time:

- 21 of 28 weekly Sunday sessions; 40 of 53 Sunday/Monday sessions; 45 of 60 Sunday/Wednesday sessions; 19 of 25 weekly Monday sessions

- After two absences, parents will be notified.

- Satisfactory completion of makeup work will compensate for missed class sessions.

- Excessive tardiness (ten or more minutes 25 percent of the time) will be treated as absence.

Promotion

Promotion to the next grade is based on documentation that the student has successfully demonstrated mastery of the required material for his or her grade level. This decision rests jointly with the classroom teacher and the educational director.

Students who need to do additional work for promotion will be assigned an appropriate activity or project. Promotion will be dependent on the satisfactory completion of the assignment.

Classroom Visits

We are delighted to have you visit your student's class during the school year. However, to avoid unscheduled interruptions or other disruptions of the school routine, we require advance notification of a visit. To arrange such a visit, please call the school office to set up a specific time and date. When you arrive at the building, please sign in with the office personnel, who will provide you with a written authorization to visit a specific classroom.

Please be aware that we have instructed all teaching staff to request written authorization from the education director (or his or her designee) before allowing an adult to visit the class. Please note: This is *not* a time for a conference. Make other arrangements for a conference if needed.

Adminis"trivia"

Dress Code

We expect all students to dress in a manner appropriate for synagogue. If students are participating in team sports immediately before or after religious school, uniforms will be allowed. However, hats, cleats, and rollerblades are not to be worn at any time during religious school. Shoes must be worn at all times.

When in the sanctuary, boys are required to wear *kipot*. Girls have the option to do so.

Traffic

For the safety of our children, we ask parents to observe carefully all standard traffic regulations. In particular, do not double-park along Bell Avenue or in the school driveway.

Do not park on Bell Avenue across from the synagogue and expect your child to cross the street to reach your car. If you need to park across the street or up the block on 27th Street, please come to the school building and walk with your child(ren) to your car.

Do not park in the handicap space unless you have legal proof of your right to do so.

Please take the time to observe standard safety guidelines. A moment of rushed carelessness is not worth injury to a child.

Pickup

Religious school staff will wait for all children to be picked up from the synagogue. Fifteen minutes after the end of class, all children still waiting will be asked to come inside the building for their safety (particularly in the evening when it is dark).

Please respect the time and commitment of the school staff as they wait with your children. Let us know if you expect to be late.

No child will be left at school unattended.

Promptness

Being on time is important. Please make certain children are in class and ready for school on time. Late arrival to class often contributes to difficulties in class. Also, please pick up children promptly, particularly in the evening.

Reporting Procedures and Parent Conferences

Teachers will report to you about your child's progress twice a year—in January and in June. In addition, if in the school's estimation your child is not achieving to the school's expectation, you will be notified by early November and early March. There will be an opportunity for you to discuss the reports with the teacher during privately scheduled conferences.

Materials

Your child has received school books as part of the school fee. Books should be covered, labeled with the child's name, and cared for as special objects. All books will be sent home at the end of the school year. We hope they will help you build a Jewish home library.

Please check to make sure your child brings all books and material to each class session.

Homework

One Congregation's Policy

It is the policy of our school that homework be assigned *each week*, in each class, grade 4 and up. Occasionally, homework will also be given in the lower grades.

Homework can take the form of reading assigned pages, completing assigned pages in a workbook, and written work of other types. Students may also be asked to bring news items from the newspaper or magazines as part of their homework.

This list of homework assignments is not inclusive. Other assignments may be devised. Teachers may assign a combination of types of homework.

In addition to the above, students in the fourth grade will also have weekly assignments in Hebrew. *All* midweek students, Hebrew and confirmation, will have assignments for each class.

One Educator's View

What about assigning homework on a regular basis in our religious schools? Obviously, religious education is not a priority in the lives of most of the families that send their children to our religious schools. Therefore, homework is even farther down on the list of priorities. In addition, many of our students are involved in numerous extracurricular and other activities after school hours. Therefore, it is suggested that with the exception of Hebrew school, homework be done on a project basis. The concept is that each class will, sometime or other during the course of the September-May school year, involve itself in one special project that will require students to do work outside the classroom. That would be the only time homework will be assigned.

Beyond Attendance Policies

To acknowledge the importance of regular attendance at religious school, it was suggested that we hold a party for those students who have a perfect attendance record. The party could be held every six weeks during the last half hour of religious school. Either at the religious school assembly marking the close of the school in the spring or at a religious school Shabbat service, attendance awards should be given to students who have two or less absences throughout the school year.

Expectations for Benei Mitzvah

At the previous board meeting the rabbi requested that board members give some thought to their expectations for bar and bat mitzvah ceremonies. The following are comments made by board members. Some were repeated many times but are only listed here once.

1. The student should be required to attend worship services.

2. The education process should make it possible for the child to function adequately on the *bimah*.

3. The ceremony is the culmination of a long period of training and education and is not a "stand alone" event.

4. The ceremony demonstrates a clear level of Hebrew language proficiency.

5. The child will be expected to be the "rabbi for the day," at the minimum conducting the full Torah service from the time that the Torah is removed from the ark until it is returned. The ceremony should also include the opportunity for the student to deliver a talk to the congregation.

6. The ceremony and the experience should focus on accomplishment, and it should be as pleasant an experience as possible for the student and the family.

7. The ceremony is to be considered the highlight of Hebrew education.

Statement on Required Service Attendance

It is the long-established policy of our congregation that students in the second and third years of midweek Hebrew and in both years of confirmation class are required to attend services with a congregation twice a month, September through May. If attendance twice in any month is not possible, please notify the rabbi in advance. The attendance that is missed *must* be made up during the following month.

Please note the following:

1. It says *services*, not just Shabbat services—so all holidays are counted.

2. Attendance is to be with a congregation—so a service provided *just* for teens at a conclave or convention does not count.

In past years, the rabbi has had to call and/or write families to prod them to meet this requirement. For the 1993-94 school year, the Religious School Committee is telling the rabbi that he is to permit *only one* month to elapse without sufficient makeup of any services that are missed before bringing the matter to the full committee. The committee has the right to remove any student from participation in the program for which he/she is attending services if the requirement is not met.

For those students who live out of town and worship regularly with another congregation, we will require a written statement from the parents each month to the effect that the requirement has been met. If any student worships with another congregation, for example, to celebrate a family bar/bat mitzvah, a written note from the parents will assure that the attendance is credited.

Those students who live out of town and worship regularly with another congregation *must attend services at our congregation at least once a month* in the final year before bar/bat mitzvah and confirmation. They may attend the other required service at their hometown congregation.

May we suggest that students who attend services without their parents are missing a great deal that such an experience can provide. Furthermore, the parent is sending the child the very clear message that services do not matter, that they are a bother, that they are for children and not for adults, and that once the requirement is over, no one from the family will be present at services. In other words, the message is:

*It doesn't matter, but we have to put up with it
to get you through bar/bat mitzvah or confirmation.*

Then, forget it.

Approved, Religious School Committee, August 18, 1993

APPENDIX B

BAR/BAT MITZVAH AND CONFIRMATION REDEFINED

Lawrence N. Mahrer

One of the first, most significant, and certainly most enduring changes instituted by our early reformers was the ceremony of confirmation for teenage boys and girls. This ceremony, with its focus on the equality of the sexes, its group or class emphasis, and its underlying theme of the acceptance of Judaism, quickly became a mainstay of Reform congregational life. Secondarily, there was a lessening of emphasis on Hebrew education and the eventual, almost total, curtailment of bar mitzvah. For early Reform Judaism, bar mitzvah was replaced by confirmation.

That this situation has changed is clear and obvious to all associated with Reform Judaism. The contrasts between the *Pittsburgh Platform* (1885) and the *Guiding Principles* (1937) make this quite clear. The *Guiding Principles* speak at length of the necessity for Hebrew education and for the use of Hebrew in synagogue and home liturgy and ritual, and they put an important emphasis on the whole field of religious education. All these things were lacking in the 1885 document. From 1937 to the present, the pace of change has only accelerated. When I was growing up in Cleveland, Ohio, the focus and goal of the religious education program of our Reform congregation was confirmation. While it was true that some of the students celebrated bar mitzvah, the emphasis was on confirmation. I cannot remember any of my friends leaving religious school after bar mitzvah. That seems to have changed significantly. The exodus of thirteen-year-old boys and girls from our congregations following bar/bat mitzvah is a steadily growing problem. We used to pride ourselves on holding our students in religious school through confirmation, and the fact that we frequently no longer do so occasions this article.

In a congregation that I once served, a new resident of the community was referred to me by our Membership Committee chairman. This resident had some questions that only I could answer. His son was about to reach his thirteenth birthday in three months, and the father wanted to know if his son would be able to observe his bar mitzvah on the Shabbat closest to his birth date. The policy of that congregation was to schedule bar or bat mitzvah at a time when the student had developed sufficient Hebrew skills, not necessarily in conjunction with a birthday.

I told the father that I would be able to give him an estimate of the amount of time required to prepare his son for bar mitzvah after I had the opportunity to evaluate the child's knowledge of Hebrew. I also indicated that I was fairly certain that even with excellent previous preparation, the boy would not be able to participate in a ceremony in three months. The family then joined the traditional synagogue in our community. Cassette tapes were used to prepare the boy for his bar mitzvah. Everybody appeared to be happy.

However, immediately prior to the High Holidays the following fall, the family joined our congregation and enrolled their son in our religious school. At that time, the father told me that although he came from a more traditional background and felt that bar mitzvah had to be associated with the thirteenth birthday, he was, in other respects, only comfortable as a member of a Reform congregation.

I am quite certain that this is a familiar story and one that has become more common over the course of the last few decades, as more families from backgrounds other than Reform are attracted to our synagogues.

At our most recent UAHC regional, I was privileged to serve on a panel dealing with the general topic of religious education. Following that workshop, representatives of three congregations came to speak to me about the subject of bar/bat mitzvah and confirmation. One congregation told me that many of those who had joined over the last ten to fifteen years share attitudes similar to those of the father in the preceding story. Another congregation was described as being unable to keep a significant number of students enrolled in religious education programs after bar/bat mitzvah. The people who spoke with me seemed to feel that the membership, mostly people who had grown up in that congregation, was confused about the changes that were taking place in Reform Judaism. Mentioned particularly was Reform's emphasis on bar/bat mitzvah and the feeling that in today's world this ceremony takes the place of confirmation, which *used to be* of prime importance in Reform Judaism. The husband-and-wife team from the third synagogue told me that for their congregation, bar/bat mitzvah was the "time of choice." By this they meant that the thirteen-year-old boys and girls were asked prior to the ceremony to "choose" to be Jews. Once they had made that choice, confirmation became unnecessary as it only represented an additional three years of religious school and a ceremony parallel to a graduation from religious education. As such, it was unimportant.

The experiences described above indicate to me that a significant change in thinking has occurred within our congregations. Bar/bat mitzvah is becoming much more important than it used to be, and confirmation is becoming less important. This attitude change results in a shrinkage in the number of students who continue their religious education after bar/bat mitzvah through confirmation. All this leads me to the conclusion that these two stages in the religious education life of our students need to be redefined.

I offer my thinking on the subject. Our first task is to make a very clear distinction between the religious education and life-cycle emphasis of these events. Through the administrative structure of our various congregations, this differentiation between bar/bat mitzvah and confirmation must be clearly delineated and then disseminated throughout the entire membership.

Bar/Bat Mitzvah Redefined

At one time in the long history of our people, a young man assumed that he was an adult at age thirteen, and his religion legitimately conferred that status upon him. This is not true in our time and place. If a child has not become a religious adult by the time of the ceremony, what then can the ceremony mean and signify?

I suggest that in modern Reform congregations, bar/bat mitzvah can *only* indicate to the student, the family, and the congregation that the student has achieved a significant, important level of Hebrew skills. These skills may be defined in terms of the ability to lead the congregation in worship adequately and knowingly and/or the ability to read adequately and then translate intelligently a small portion from the Torah. In our religious education programs, our Hebrew schools should meet often during the week for a sufficient number of years to make the above goals attainable. Furthermore, the emphasis in the Hebrew school should not be on bar/bat mitzvah preparation. The reason for the existence of the school is to teach Hebrew skills. The program should be of the highest possible quality, and it should be voluntary. In this way, no child is "forced" to participate, and all students realize that they are enrolled to acquire language ability. It should be clearly stated that the school is open to students who have no intention of participating in the bar/bat mitzvah ceremony. The education program is for its own sake, and the participation in a bar/bat mitzvah ceremony is a thoroughly enjoyable and meaningful by-product.

By placing the emphasis on Hebrew education rather than on the participation in the ceremony, we remove some of the stumbling blocks that are presently confusing our students and their families. In the first place, we have indicated that Hebrew study is a value in its own right. If we are successful, we are reminding our membership of the primary importance of the Hebrew language in our historical and ever-developing religious heritage. Second, if the emphasis of the education program is on participation in the ceremony, we cannot complain very much if our students "drop out" after they have reached the culminating experience. For, after all, we taught them that the ceremony was a conclusion.

Although Rabbi Hayim Halevy Donin is an Orthodox rabbi and is referring only to bar mitzvah, he voices similar thinking:

> If your son asks you the reason for his having to go to Hebrew
> school, please never say "in order to become bar mitzvah." Why?
> First, it practically closes the door in advance for studying beyond
> bar mitzvah. If your son's only reason for going to Hebrew school
> is to prepare for a bar mitzvah ceremony, then your son is led to
> believe right from the start that nothing beyond bar mitzvah is
> important or necessary. Second, it is not long before the youngster
> comes to realize that he really doesn't have to know that much for
> the bar mitzvah ceremony itself. Children are quite capable of
> quickly learning the necessary blessings and the biblical chapter of
> the Prophets by rote and of reciting them "beautifully." If the bar
> mitzvah ceremony is the goal, the mere ability to read Hebrew,
> which the child learned to do during his first year *in* Hebrew
> school, supplemented by a five- or six-month training period con-
> sisting of one hour a week is all the training he needs.

To Raise a Jewish Child, Basic Books, 1977, pp. 113-114

My material is written from my educational perspective, namely to prepare Hebrew school students to be able to participate as leaders of congregational worship and occasional readers of Torah. If the Hebrew language-skill goal of the school involves spoken Hebrew as a major portion of its focus, then in order for the bar/bat mitzvah ceremony to be a public demonstration of the student's having acquired that level of Hebrew competence, he/she should be expected to utilize the ability to speak Hebrew during the ceremony. This may take the form of a brief talk, written by the student and delivered in both Hebrew and English. Or it may take the form of a spoken dialogue between the student and the rabbi, the educator, or the student's Hebrew teacher.

Whatever format is used, the important point to remember is that the bar/bat mitzvah ceremony can be distinct and unique in our congregations only when the Hebrew skill/knowledge/competency component is emphasized. Congregants need to be informed that not all families are interested in having their children develop these language facilities. Families should also be informed that some students will learn Hebrew but will not participate in a bar/bat mitzvah ceremony. Our congregants and their children who fall into both these categories need to be supported by the professional staff of the synagogue and by its lay administrative bodies.

Confirmation Redefined

If a congregation is successful in the redefinition of its Hebrew education program and the bar/bat mitzvah ceremony, then it should also redefine confirmation. If students do not become "adults" at age thirteen, if students do not take their Judaism seriously at age thirteen, if students do not "choose" to be Jews at age thirteen, when do they experience these things? At the time of confirmation! From my point of view, confirmation becomes spiritually, psychologically, and educationally important to our students when they realize that it is the formal opportunity to declare a choice publicly. The real question is: How do we teach that understanding to our total membership?

As in the case of bar/bat mitzvah, rabbinic and other professional leadership and the lay administrative bodies of the congregation need to be totally involved in the redefinition process of confirmation. Their total support in leadership roles within our synagogues is necessary. Decisions cannot be made in matters of this nature exclusively by the professional staff. To some extent, these are "policy matters," and our religious education committees and our boards of trustees must discuss the issues thoroughly and make the decisions that create these congregational educational policies.

What I am about to describe is the method I have employed for twenty years or more in the congregations that I have served. As students enter our Hebrew school program, the goals of that program, as outlined above, are discussed with them and their parents. Throughout the Hebrew education years, students are continually reminded of the fact that their bat/bar mitzvah ceremony will be the first demonstration of their acquired Hebrew skills. They are told that they are expected to continue their religious education through confirmation. As the time for bar/bat mitzvah approaches, the significance of confirmation is discussed with the students and their parents.

We make every effort to be certain that they understand the distinction between these two life-cycle events. In more recent years, following the lead of Rabbi Haskell M. Bernat, formerly of Temple Israel of Greater Miami, I have utilized a document entitled "The Covenant of Torah" as the basis for these discussions with the family. That document says in part:

The Torah scroll is first placed into our hands at bar/bat mitzvah. Our lips speak its words, and they become implanted in our hearts. As we mature, the words of Torah and its *mitzvot* take on ever-greater meaning. This is expressed in the ceremony of confirmation. We understand both life moments are the way that a young Jew clings to Torah as a "Tree of Life." One is a prelude to the next.

Approximately a week prior to the bar/bat mitzvah ceremony, I arrange a special meeting with the student and the parents. At that meeting, we go over the content of " The Covenant of Torah" once again. We make certain that everyone understands its implication and we all sign it in the appropriate places. The student signs after a paragraph in which a promise is made to continue Jewish education at least through confirmation. The parents sign after a paragraph that indicates their willingness to support their child in the decision to continue religious education, and the rabbi signs after a statement pledging the congregation to support the child and the parents in the commitment to religious education that they have made. At the bar/bat mitzvah ceremony, the original of the document is given to the student and a copy is kept in my file.

Once a student reaches the confirmation class, which for me has always been a two-year program beginning in the ninth grade, further explanations relative to confirmation are made to both parents and students. I understand confirmation as a time of personal choice. The potential confirmand is told that at the end of two years of study, he/she will be given the choice whether or not to participate in the confirmation ceremony. I do everything in my power to see that peer pressure and parental coercion are minimized so that the individual student is as free as possible to choose to participate. It is my goal to have the students understand, prior to the actual preparation for the ceremony, that they are being asked to duplicate what their ancestors did at Sinai. They are being asked to enter into the covenant between God and the children of Israel. I repeatedly say to them something along the following lines:

> At the time of confirmation, you are asked to make a personal choice. You are asked whether or not you wish to declare publicly your affiliation with and your allegiance to the Jewish people. You are asked whether or not you wish to take your place in the unbroken chain of our tradition that stretches from the present back to Sinai. Because most of you will say yes, the confirmation ceremony always takes place on the holiday of Shavuot, which celebrates the Sinai experience.

As your rabbi, I am saying to you that I want you to make

your decision based on your present level of maturity and your present understanding of what being Jewish means to you individually. Your congregation has provided you with an opportunity to acquire a Jewish education. Your congregation has provided you with the opportunity to participate in Jewish worship. Your congregation has provided you with additional opportunities for Jewish experiences and contacts through its encouragement of your participation in Jewish summer camping and in our temple youth group. Based on those opportunities, and on what you now understand Judaism to mean, your congregation asks you to make this important choice.

My students clearly understand, as do their parents, that should they choose not to participate in the ceremony, I will strongly support that decision. In my career, it has happened only once, and that student explained that he simply did not feel ready. He did elect to participate in the confirmation ceremony a year later. To the best of my knowledge, everyone in his family and in our congregation understood his decision and supported him.

Since confirmation is the time of "choice," that aspect must be reflected in the content of the confirmation service itself. While the number of students who participate in the ceremony will have an impact on the role that any one individual can play, the total effect of the ceremony needs to convey the emotional and spiritual emphasis of choice. For example, my students have frequently utilized readings from the first chapter of Ruth for their *haftarah* because the "choice" of becoming a Jew is so clearly expressed in the words that Ruth speaks to Naomi. Likewise, most of the time my students elect to read the Ten Commandments from Exodus 20 as the Torah portion for the service. However, on two or three occasions, the students selected other narrative portions of the Sinai story that they felt better expressed the choosing aspect of confirmation. On occasion, creative liturgy, written by confirmands, has been utilized, giving the students the opportunity to express a personal choice that confirmation brings to the fore. Students have likewise delivered short talks about what it is that they have "chosen" by participating in the confirmation experience.

Not all the confirmands had participated in bar/bat mitzvah ceremonies three years earlier. Whether they had or hadn't seems to make no significant difference except for their ability to handle some of the Hebrew included in the service. Those who had participated in the Hebrew study program, whether leading to bar/bat mitzvah or not, were obviously better qualified than those who had not. Teenagers who had participated in the bar/bat mitzvah ceremonies seem to be a little less frightened by confirmation and seem to have somewhat more poise while on the *bimah*.

When I was a teenager growing up in Cleveland, it was common to say, "I was confirmed at...," and we would fill in the name of the congregation. In my case, I said, "I was confirmed at Brickner's temple." Now, because of the element of choice, which I so strongly emphasize, I insist that my students say, "I participated in confirmation at...." In other words, I am trying to help my students understand that confirmation is not something "bestowed" by a rabbi but is something that the teenager does for himself/herself.

It is obvious from the above that as a rabbi, I am highly involved with my confirmation students. I firmly believe that the success of the confirmation program requires this level of rabbinic participation. If the students are to appreciate fully the seriousness of the choice that the rabbi and the congregation are asking them to make, they need to see and experience the dedication and involvement of the rabbi. It is obvious that the rabbi must be at least one of the teachers, if not the only teacher, for confirmation class. The students need the opportunity for a long-term relationship with their rabbi so they can have the opportunity of getting to know each other.

The teenager needs to come into contact with an adult Jew who is fully committed to Judaism and who has made some significant personal choices about Judaism. The rabbi is a good example. My experience has taught me that students who like their rabbi and enjoy being in the company of their rabbi also learn to enjoy their Jewishness and their experience with the synagogue and religious education. Many students who are "divorced" from their rabbi find it more difficult to develop positive attitudes toward religious education, confirmation, the synagogue, and Jewish life.

Of course, the rabbi need not be the only adult fully committed to Judaism with whom our potential confirmands may come into contact. I fondly remember a teacher in the religious school of my youth, Mamie Raymar, who had a profound influence on me. A congregation's educator, cantor, administrator, and/or youth group adviser may be the person chosen by the student. However, because of the relationship of the rabbi to the confirmation ceremony, I feel that he/she has the most definitive role to play.

If, as described, confirmation is the time for making choices, as congregations we need to provide opportunities for our students to begin to exercise options. We cannot rely on our students' homes because they are environments created and controlled by adults. Within the structure of the synagogue, a properly run youth group will give teenagers the option of choice.

If we were to attempt to categorize those areas in which Jews make significant personal, religious choices, our list may include: education, worship/ritual, social action, community service, and personal ethics. However long the list might be, it can become an outline for TYG programming and function.

Conclusion

I believe that the role of the rabbi is critical. I further believe that we rabbis need to analyze our priorities when deciding to what extent we will participate in the classes leading to confirmation and how much we intend to interact with our high school youth groups. It is unfortunate that so many rabbis consider themselves to be so busy that they cannot find time to spend with their potential confirmands. Our congregants and students are confused about bar/bat mitzvah and confirmation. They need not be. Solutions do exist that only require a rethinking of the significance of the two life-cycle events. The suggestions presented here are intended to initiate that redefinition process.

APPENDIX C

TZEDAKAH

Where the Money Goes and Why

Lawrence N. Mahrer

In the spring of 1983, one of our larger congregations ran an article in its bulletin, which included the following:

> The Keren Ami Council will meet with Rabbi _____ to select the organizations to which the Keren Ami monies collected from our students this year will be distributed. The council consists of one student elected from each classroom, grades four through confirmation....

The article went on to describe how the students were elected, how they would determine the donation recipients, and the total amount already collected. The article further stated that once the decisions are made, a detailed report will be published in a later issue of the bulletin.

This is the same method and process that was in use in the 1940s when I was a student in religious school. The end result is that the vast majority of the students in the school are completely unaware of the nature, needs, and worthiness of the organizations to which their nickels, dimes, and quarters are finally sent. An entirely different method of collecting and distributing *tzedakah is* possible, and I believe it to be much more educationally sound. The concept is to educate the children in the school about the organization *as they are collecting money for it.*

The process begins at some point in the school year when the oldest class devotes a portion of a class session to creating a long list of potential organizations to receive the *tzedakah* monies. This selection activity should, if possible, include the parents as well, thus involving them in the religious education process of the congregation. Once this list has been created, each student is assigned to learn as much about one individual organization as possible in the week between classes. The student prepares for the class an explanation of the services the organization provides, the clientele it serves, and its needs. That student should also be prepared to advocate for the organization in the final selection process the following week.

At the next session of the class, the students discuss all the potential recipients on their list and select the six or seven to which they will donate during the ensuing school year. In this final selection step, two criteria must be met: At least one-half of the organizations must be Jewish in nature and at least one-half must be local, meaning that some of their work must be carried out in the community in which the students live.

These two criteria were developed because this whole process is designed to assist students in learning about *tzedakah* and about needs and services. Over the years, our students should become aware of the various types of services provided under Jewish auspices, and they should learn considerably more about the variety of needs that are being met in their own communities. Experience has indicated that this element of learning about the human and social requirements of their *own* communities has been very interesting and stimulating for students. In fact, at least one student has been motivated to become directly involved as a volunteer with one of the organizations for which we collected *tzedakah* based on what was studied in religious school.

Once the specific organizations have been selected, they should be contacted, informed that the students will be collecting money for them, and asked for their cooperation. Their involvement might take a variety of forms, depending upon staff availability, the extent of printed and audiovisual materials they have produced, and their willingness to cooperate. Every organization contacted over the years in which this program has been in operation has been very willing to help us educate our students about what they do and how and why they do it. In selecting each individual who will make a contact, the educator has some options. If the students are mature enough, they can contact the organizations. If not, the contact can be made by the rabbi, the educator or principal, or the congregational office.

Recipient organizations are requested to provide printed materials to be handed out to our students. Frequently, organizations have prepared items that are already age-graded. Some materials are solicited for use by our classroom teachers; others can be taken home by our students for their parents. It is our desire to inform the parents about the various organizations in the hope that they will be motivated to contribute to them or, at the very least, learn about them. The organizations are also requested to provide audiovisual materials that can be used in assembly programs and/or speakers to visit our school.

In our initial contact with the organization, we inquire if there is a specific item of equipment they need that our students might be able to purchase for them. For example, one mental health institution needed some additional athletic supplies that their county budget could not afford. Our students decided to buy whatever was possible with the money we raised for them. Whenever we exercised this option, we first ascertained that the item to be purchased was in some way meaningful to our students. For example, children could relate to athletic equipment, whereas they could not relate to the purchase of office supplies.

During the five or six weeks that we collect money on behalf of a specific organization, classroom teachers are requested to discuss the organization, what it does, whom it serves, why its needs exist, etc. This is done weekly, using the materials the organization has provided for us. Material to be sent home with the students is staggered throughout the collection period. Speakers and audiovisual materials are used at the beginning of the process and again, if available, during the middle as a second-stage motivator.

At each assembly, the students are informed about the amount collected that week and the total amount to date. This also becomes a motivating factor because it gives us another opportunity to talk about the organization without repeating what has already been presented to the students in their classrooms. If a specific goal for an organization has been set, the assembly discussion provides a chance to relate what has been raised toward that goal.

When we are finished raising money for a particular organization, there are options for the next step. If the organization is local and our students have decided to purchase something for it, a presentation ceremony can be arranged. This presentation can take place during an assembly program for the whole school or in the presence of the entire congregation at a Shabbat service. If possible, some of the students may even visit the organization to deliver the gift personally. This was done for a home for the aged, where the students also presented a program of Israeli songs and dances for the residents.

The purpose of the step described above is to keep student interest high, to provide a final opportunity for students to learn about the organization, and to help them feel good about themselves and what they have accomplished. Furthermore, we are attempting to teach our students that these organizations need people as well as money to help them and that money alone is not sufficient. If we can involve our students with the organization in some meaningful and satisfying way, over the course of years we can introduce our students to the *mitzvah* of service.

If a special presentation for an organization cannot take place, a detailed letter to the organization accompanies our check. The letter explains our program and asks for a letter in return that commends our students and their efforts and repeats some of the information about the organization that they have already learned. Thus, when the organization's response is photocopied and read in classrooms or the assembly, it becomes a reminder of the students' achievements and a final educational tool about the recipient of our *tzedakah*.

Articles in our congregational bulletin tell the membership something about each of the organizations for which we collected. At the end of each individual campaign, we report the total raised for that organization and announce the next campaign.

On occasion, we have kept this *tzedakah* money in a separate pass-book account with weekly deposits made. One year, it was even possible to have the students manage this account. We have at times used one or two Sundays to raise additional money for a special need that might arise or for an additional contribution to an organization our students feel is worthy of more than they have collected.

At times, the need to conduct special campaigns does arise. For instance, in May 1983, Topeka was struck by a tornado late on a Friday afternoon. On the following Sunday, our students suggested that we hold a special *tzedakah* campaign the following week to aid the victims of the storm. The result was outstanding: eight to nine times the amount generally collected on a Sunday. The money was immediately given to one of the organizations chosen by our students from among the many providing aid.

A few years ago, we had a student whose father had received some assistance from the organization about which we were then studying and for which we were raising money. That student suggested to classmates that a bake sale be held to increase the contribution we were making to that organization. With the assistance of the teacher and the room parents, this was accomplished, and the entire congregation was able to participate in this school *tzedakah* project.

In both cases discussed above, the initial idea came from our students. Student involvement in the program and the constant discussion of the organizations in classrooms and assemblies succeeded in instilling in the students a sense of caring and responsibility. Thus we had achieved some of our educational goals for our students.

APPENDIX D

A MERGED RELIGIOUS SCHOOL

Bet Shalom Religious School: A Merged School for a Reform and a Conservative Congregation in Neighboring Communities

Bet Shalom Religious School began as a response to two synagogues that were simultaneously experiencing decreased enrollment and difficulty finding teachers in the late 1970s. In the neighboring communities of Racine and Kenosha, Wisconsin, members of Racine's Beth Israel Sinai and Kenosha's Beth Hillel sometimes came into contact with one another and shared mutual concerns about their children. Based on these concerns, the two schools began initially to plan occasional "exchange" mornings. The two congregations' school committees then decided to seriously consider a merger. This was in 1980. The first step was to call a meeting in each congregation with the parents of all school-aged children to share the idea of the merger and to receive feedback. Soon thereafter, a joint school committee consisting of members from the two congregations was formed to plan the merger. The original "Letter of Agreement," which provides governance for this committee and other policies for the merged school, follows on pages 79-81.

Since one congregation is Reform and the other Conservative, initial issues revolved around curriculum, how to handle the bar/bat mitzvah and confirmation programs, whether to use Ashkenazic or Sephardic Hebrew, and whether *kipot* would be required in the sanctuary. Other issues under consideration were where the school would meet, what textbooks to use, and how to divide the cost of running the school in an equitable manner, since one congregation had considerably fewer students than the other.

The problems were resolved as follows: Only the Sunday morning religious schools were merged. Hebrew school, bar/bat mitzvah, and confirmation were kept under the purview of the individual congregations. The school would meet half of each year in each building, moving midyear so that materials would need to be moved only once a year. This enabled the school to stay in one location for an entire year and to split the winter-driving burden in half. This also made it possible to celebrate holidays in both synagogues (e.g., one year the school would be in Racine for Sukot and the next year in Kenosha). The issue of *kipot* was settled by observing *minhag hamakom* in each synagogue. Books from each school were inventoried and then combined. The curriculum was put together by a subcommittee of the combined school committee, using elements from the existing curricula from each congregation. The curriculum has been revised a few times as new rabbis came into the picture.

Funding the school was a more complicated issue, but it was worked out according to a formula that satisfied all. After an annual budget was established and a tuition fee agreed upon, the shortfall between expenses and income would be covered by the two congregations. The individual congregations would determine the manner in which their contribution would be financed. (For a time, in fact, this meant that one congregation charged its families additional tuition while the other did not.) It was agreed that half of this remaining cost would be evenly split by the two congregations. The other half would be paid by the congregations on a per capita basis. Thus, the congregation that had more children would pay more of this second half, and the congregation that had fewer children would pay less. The thinking behind this division of the remaining costs was that there are some costs that are fixed no matter how many children there are. There are other costs (e.g., supplies, books, and food) that are clearly determined by numbers. This plan has now worked successfully for fourteen years, even though the number of childeren enrolled in the program from each congregation has shifted.

In spite of the merger, we still combine grades to achieve larger classes, requiring fewer teachers. At one point, the school added a preschool program, and at this time there are six classes: preschool (ages three and four), K-1, 2-3, 4-5, 6-7, and 8-10.

Initially, there were a few disgruntled families who were annoyed because of the additional distance. Efforts were made to arrange car pools to help people who felt especially inconvenienced. Soon after the school was established, most people realized that the driving was not a great inconvenience. Yet today the distance is still occasionally an issue. For example, over the last three years, the post-benei mitzvah age class requested to meet at a separate time over pizza. This has created a situation in which some families must drive twice in one day because they have children in different age groups. We settled this issue by having the 8-10 class meet in the city in which the school was *not* meeting that semester so that Kenosha families had to drive only once a day to Racine and vice versa. (The distance between the two cities is about ten miles, but it can be a one-half hour drive from certain neighborhoods.)

Over the years, there have been occasional intercongregational flare-ups at school committee meetings. This has happened particularly when there were new rabbis who wanted to change the status quo. Such situations have been resolved by reviewing and reaffirming the need for and the value of the concept of the merged school. The issues have been settled with the best interest of the students and the preservation of the school in mind.

Since the beginning, the school has hired an administrator to do the detailed work of obtaining supplies, keeping records, sending notices, staffing the office on Sunday mornings, and so on. The rabbis' roles have varied over the years, depending on their interests and capabilities. The rabbis have shared the responsibility of text decisions, curriculum writing and implementation, interviewing, preparing and advising teachers, and teaching the upper grade classes. Both rabbis are in the school each week and divide the responsibilities for the two weekly services (upper grades and lower grades). The rabbis also plan special events and parent programs.

Although I have tried to cover as many aspects of the school as possible, I am sure this summary is incomplete. I would be happy to answer questions for anyone seeking to implement such an undertaking.

Dena A. Feingold
Rabbi, Beth Hillel Temple
Kenosha, Wisconsin

Bet Shalom Religious School

Kenosha-Racine, Wisconsin

LETTER OF AGREEMENT

In May 1980, the congregations of Beth Israel Sinai Temple, Racine, Wisconsin, and Beth Hillel Temple, Kenosha, Wisconsin, came to recognize that they shared certain problems, particularly in the area of Jewish religious education. Among those problems were declining enrollment, difficulty in finding faculty, and poor utilization of resources. With that realization, the two congregations established a combined Sunday morning religious school.

The school is known by the name Bet Shalom Religious School. It is an entity unto itself, separate and distinct from both congregations. It serves only families that belong to one of the two congregations. Both congregations agree that neither congregation shall withdraw unilaterally from all parts or any part of this program.

Having established this school, the two congregations have maintained and improved the quality of Jewish religious education; have provided enrichment for the children and families of the two congregations; have used resources better and have tried to provide social interaction among the children and families of these small relatively isolated communities. While the cost of a combined school may be lower than that for separate schools, it was, and should continue to be, understood that the school was not established for the purpose of lowering costs.

School Government

The governing body of the school is a committee comprised of four representatives from each congregation. In addition, the president and rabbi of each congregation, as well as the administrator, shall be ex-officio members of the committee, without a vote.

The chairperson of the committee shall alternate between the congregations every two years. The committee shall elect a secretary and treasurer annually. The secretary shall see that the minutes and reports are submitted to the president of each congregation. The treasurer shall sign all checks and be responsible for a continual audit of school finances.

Committee meetings shall be held in response to need or desire. The duties of the committee shall be, within the limits of the bylaws of both congregations, to set fees, establish an annual budget, determine curriculum, create a school calendar, hire faculty, and formulate all policies and standards for the operation of the school. These policies and standards shall include, but not be limited to, homework, attendance, discipline, promptness, schedule, and parent communication.

Financial Arrangements

The annual budget for the operation of the school shall be prepared by the committee as early as possible during the spring of the previous academic year. This budget shall be submitted to the boards of each congregation for advice and consent.

Letter of Agreement

Based on this budget, each congregation shall be responsible for a set fee for each child registered, plus half of all costs in excess of those fees.

The school shall maintain its own checking account. The administrator of the school shall have authority to make purchases of amounts up to $75.00. All purchases in excess of this amount must be approved by the committee.

Administrative Considerations

The school shall meet for half of each academic year in each temple. The school shall change locations annually, either at midyear or in the January immediately following winter recess, as the committee shall determine.

All textbooks and audiovisual hardware and software now owned by both congregations shall be made available to the school. Students and faculty shall have access to the library of each congregation.

The school shall be responsible for all materials that are used. New purchases shall be made by the school and become the property of the school.

The committee shall hire an administrator for the school. The administrator shall be responsible for all communications with parents, teachers, students, and the committee. Other duties of the administrator shall include coordination of in-service training, of all religious school programs, and of all materials; administration of school policies; and maintenance of all school records.

The role of the rabbis shall include, but not be limited to, teacher supervision, teaching, supervision of worship services, curriculum development, providing Jewish enrichment content, and serving as resource persons to the school.

Mutual Considerations

We recognize that this school includes people who come from a variety of backgrounds, with their own customs and traditions. The school was established to serve the needs of two congregations, each with its own traditions and its own approach to Jewish religious law. It is the policy of the school to respect all such approaches and traditions equally and to encourage mutual respect among all concerned.

Approved and accepted 13 April 1993
For Beth Hillel Temple _____
(signed)

Approved and accepted 26 April 1993
For Beth Israel Sinai Temple _____
(signed)

APPENDIX E

ADMINISTRATION

EDUCATIONAL GOALS

Goals of the Congregation
Tifereth Jacob Education Program

The School Board of Congregation Tifereth Jacob affirms that the strength and welfare of the Jewish people and Congregation Tifereth Jacob are inextricably bound to the Jewish education of our people. From its earliest beginnings, the Jewish tradition has required that the laws, customs, and ceremonies of our people be transmitted from generation to generation. The very fabric of Jewish life—from the public reading of the Torah to the retelling of the Exodus at the seder table to the requirement of daily study—is focused on the ideals of Jewish education.

We believe that our school program should educate and equip our children to develop a love of Judaism that will enrich their lives through adulthood. Our programs engender an identification with the Jewish community and Israel, an enrichment of the Jewish home, and a commitment to Jewish ethical behavior and values. The school program should prepare and motivate students to practice Judaism out of respect and love for its traditions, as well as their knowledge of its history, language, and rituals.

The Goals of our Religious Education Program

1. To imbue the student with love of God and trust in God's goodness

2. To provide opportunities for the child to develop spiritual and ethical sensitivity through curricular experiences

3. To foster a positive Jewish identity within the student

4. To integrate the student's Jewish experiences with those of the synagogue community

5. To develop basic Jewish literacy, including study of Hebrew, siddur skills, Torah, Jewish history, and to teach the importance of observing Jewish rituals and holidays

6. To develop personal religious thought and creative spiritual expression, as well as skills in Jewish prayer

7. To emphasize the concept of *mitzvah* as a basis for Jewish belief and action

8. To provide focused opportunities for family involvement in order to enhance and encourage independent Jewish family life

9. To create an appreciation of lifelong Torah study as a vital link to our tradition

10. To develop a kinship with *K'lal Yisrael*, the "world Jewish community," by actively seeking the welfare of Jews throughout the world and to affirm our historical bond to *Eretz Yisrael*, the "Land of Israel"

RELIGIOUS SCHOOL FAMILY CALENDAR

Please note that the sample calendar below includes a wide range of notations that do not coincide with the days when the religious school was in session. It is our feeling that each holiday needs to be listed, as do special congregational events and secular holidays and observances. I hope that the classroom teacher will discuss everything listed on the calendar for the coming week, attempting to relate secular events to Jewish values.

IF THE DATE HAS A NUMBER PRECEDING IT, RELIGIOUS SCHOOL MEETS!

This calendar includes everything we believe a family of our students should know about during the school year. All sessions are at 10 A.M. Vacation dates are based on the Florence, South Carolina, District 1 calendar.

Monday, September 5	EREV ROSH HASHANAH, 8:00 P.M.
Tuesday, September 6	ROSH HASHANAH, 10:00 A.M.
	Children's Services, 2:30 P.M.
1. Sunday, September 11	FIRST SESSION—Opening Activities
	Cemetery Memorial Service, 1:30 P.M.
Wednesday, September 14	KOL NIDRE, 8:00 P.M.
Thursday, September 15	YOM KIPPUR, 10:00 A.M.
	Children's Services, 1:30 P.M.
	Afternoon Services, 2:30 P.M.
2. Sunday, September 18	SUKAH DECORATING— OUR CONGREGATION
Monday, September 19	EREV SUKOT FAMILY SERVICE, 7:00 P.M.
3. Sunday, September 25	
Monday, September 26	EREV SIMCHAT TORAH/ CONSECRATION SERVICE, 7:00 P.M.
4. Sunday, October 2	
5. Sunday, October 9	
Monday, October 10	COLUMBUS DAY
6. Sunday, October 16	

84

7. Sunday, October 23	
Monday, October 24	UNITED NATIONS DAY
8. Sunday, October 30	David Syme Piano Concert, 3:00 P.M.
Sunday, November 6	*NO SCHOOL*
Tuesday, November 8	ELECTION DAY
Friday, November 11	VETERANS DAY
9. Sunday, November 13	Skating Party
10. Sunday, November 20	
Friday, November 25	THANKSGIVING FAMILY SERVICE, 7:30 P.M.
Sunday, November 27	*NO SCHOOL*
	FIRST LIGHT OF CHANUKAH
11. Sunday, December 4	CHANUKAH PARTY—AFTER CLASS, 11:00 A.M.
	LAST LIGHT OF CHANUKAH
Saturday, December 10	HUMAN RIGHTS DAY
12. Sunday, December 11	
Thursday, December 15	BILL OF RIGHTS DAY
Sunday, December 18	*NO SCHOOL*
Sunday, December 25	*NO SCHOOL*
Sunday, January 1	*NO SCHOOL*
13. Sunday, January 8	Sale of Trees Begins
14. Sunday, January 15	
Monday, January 16	MARTIN LUTHER KING, JR., DAY
	TU BISHVAT
15. Sunday, January 22	
16. Sunday, January 29	Last Day of Tree Sale
17. Sunday, February 5	TV Game Day—11:00 A.M.
18. Sunday, February 12	
Tuesday, February 14	RACE RELATIONS DAY
Friday, February 17	11th Annual "Neighbor Night"
19. Sunday, February 19	
20. Sunday, February 26	
21. Sunday, March 5	

22. Sunday, March 12
    Wednesday, March 15   EREV PURIM SERVICE, 7:00 P.M.
    Friday, March 17   BAR MITZVAH—
                           Aaron Brown, 8:00 P.M.
23. Sunday, March 19   PURIM PARTY—AFTER CLASS
24. Sunday, March 26
25. Sunday, April 2
    Sunday, April 9   *NO SCHOOL*
    Friday, April 14   EREV PESACH—HOME SEDER
    Saturday, April 15   PESACH SERVICE, 10:30 A.M.
    Sunday, April 16   *NO SCHOOL*
    Friday, April 21   PESACH YISKOR, 8:00 P.M.
26. Sunday, April 23
    Thursday, April 27   YOM HASHOAH
27. Sunday, April 30
    Thursday, May 4   YOM HA'ATZMAUT
    Saturday, May 6   BAT MITZVAH—Laura Greenberg
28. Sunday, May 7
29. Sunday, May 14   MOTHER'S DAY
    Friday, May 19   RELIGIOUS SCHOOL SHABBAT,
                           7:30 P.M.
30. Sunday, May 21   LAST SESSION—SPECIAL EVENT
    Sunday, June 4   SHAVUOT/CONFIRMATION,
                           10:30 A.M.
    Saturday, June 10   BAR MITZVAH—Jonathan Drucker
    Sunday, June 18   FATHER'S DAY

SAMPLE FORMS

New Student Registration

Temple Israel Religious School

(*Returning students need not complete this form.*)

Student's Name _____
                        (First)   (Middle Initial)   (Last)

Student's Hebrew Name _____

Student's Date of Birth _____ Age _____

Secular School Grade Level _____ School Attending _____

Religious School Last Attended _____

Address of School   _____

                           _____

                           _____

Has your child been consecrated? _____ If so, when? _____
(Consecration takes place at Simchat Torah services; children receive a certificate
and a miniature Torah.)

* *

Please list names and ages of siblings.

_____

_____

_____

_____

* *

If you are registering for Hebrew school:

Any previous Hebrew study? _____ How many years? _____

What texts were used? _____

When are you planning to have a bar/bat mitzvah? _____

Shabbat Service Attendance Report

Note that it is preferred, not requested, that this report be completed about a service or ceremony that takes place somewhere other than Congregation Tifereth Jacob. This suggestion is made in order to encourage families to encounter a variety of Jewish worship experiences.

Name _____ Grade _____

Location of Service/Ceremony _____

Date of Service/Ceremony _____

1. What was the purpose of the service or ceremony? (Shabbat, bar/bat mitzvah, baby naming, wedding, funeral, something else) _____
_____

2. Who conducted the service? (rabbi, cantor, someone else) _____
_____

3. Did anyone else help lead the service? _____ If so, what types of activities did this person help lead? _____
_____

4. Was there a Torah reading? _____ If so, what was the Torah portion about? _____
_____

5. Did someone deliver a sermon or a talk? _____ If so, what did he/she want you to learn?
_____
_____

6. Why do we have this type of service in our Jewish tradition?
_____
_____

7. Why do we get together as a congregation or group for this type of service?
_____

Parent's Signature _____

Progress Report 5750

Temple Beth El Religious School

Student's Name _____ Grade _____

Teacher _____ Term: Fall

Attendance _____ Present out of _____ Sessions

	Excellent		Above Average		Average		Below Average		Needs Improvement	
	Heb	Jud	Heb	Jud	Heb	Jud	Heb	Jud	Heb	Jud
Participation in class activities										
Cooperation with teacher											
Cooperation with peers											
Class preparation/ homework											
Mastery of class material											

Additional Teacher Comments: _____
_____
_____
_____

Student's Comments: _____
_____
_____

Parent's Comments and Signature: _____
_____
_____
_____

_____   _____
Teacher's Signature   Educator's Signature

Weekly Report to Parents

Beth Israel Congregation
Florence, South Carolina

A. This section of the report is to be completed by the student with help from the teacher.

Date _____ to the parents of _____

In class today we learned about

1.

2.

3.

4.

Please talk to me about these things so that *you* can learn about them and help me remember them.

My homework assignment for next week is _____

_____

_____

_____

B. This section of the report is to be completed by the teacher. These are the teacher's comments on your child:

❑ 1. Participated well in class discussion

❑ 2. Was helpful to his/her classmates

❑ 3. Came to class prepared, with homework completed

❑ 4. Listened well and followed directions

❑ 5. Seemed interested in our class work

❑ 6. Behaved very well

Student Progress Report
Primary Department

Temple Beth Hillel Religious School

Student's Name _____ Teacher _____

Semester _____ Grade _____ Room _____

Attendance: Days Present _____ Days Absent _____

Excellent = E	Has Shown Improvement = SI
Satisfactory = S	Needs Improvement = NI

PROGRESS IN JUDAIC STUDIES
1. Able to recognize and recall basic concepts _____
2. Able to define key terms _____
3. Able to give examples within the major areas of study _____
4. Able to offer opinions about topics studied _____

DEMONSTRATION OF HEBREW-READINESS SKILLS
1. Recognizes Hebrew letters _____
2. Recalls key vocabulary _____
3. Able to participate in *Tefilah* (prayer service) _____

PARTICIPATION AND CONDUCT
1. Cooperates with others _____
2. Listens to teachers and classmates _____
3. Follows instructions _____
4. Respects property _____
5. Participates in discussion and activities _____
6. Completes homework assignments _____

Comments and Recommendations

_____

_____

_____

_____

_____   _____
Teacher's Signature   Educator's Signature

APPENDIX F

DISCIPLINE POLICIES

Covenant of Conduct

Temple Israel Religious School

Temple Israel Religious School is a *bet mikdash,* a "sanctuary," as well as a *bet midrash,* a "house of study." Our children must know they are in a safe environment to study, worship, learn, and play. In order to realize these goals, we ask each student's family to read and discuss this "Covenant of Conduct," sign it, and return it to the office along with the registration materials.

Treat others kindly.
Rabbi Shammai said: Receive all people with a cheerful face.

Pay close attention to each other's words and feelings.
Rabbi Hillel said: What you don't like, don't do to your neighbor.

Respect the property of others.
Rabbi Yossi said: Let the property of your neighbor be as precious as your own.

Be responsible for your behavior.
Rabi said: Which is the right path to choose? One that is honorable in itself and also wins honor for others.

Make a positive effort.
Ben Hei Hei said: According to the labor is the reward.

We have read this "Covenant of Conduct," have discussed it as a family, and agree to abide by it in order to create the best possible learning environment.

_____   _____
Student   Date

_____   _____
Parent   Parent

Religious School Conduct Guidelines

Beth Israel Congregation
Florence, South Carolina

In order to help us create a conducive learning atmosphere for your children and all our students, the Religious School Committee is asking all parents to discuss the following conduct guidelines with their children, sign it as indicated, and *return it to the school with registration fees or at the first session of classes.*

1. All students are expected to be in their classrooms, in their seats, when school begins at 10:00 A.M. When going to their classrooms, students are expected to walk.

2. Hats and coats are to be removed and hung on the hooks in the hall or on the back of student seats.

3. Running, the use of "outside voices," rudeness, improper language, fighting (even when thought to be in "play"), and the lack of courtesy for other students and adults are always inappropriate in our school.

4. Unless arranged by the teacher or with the teacher in advance, food is not to be brought to school.

5. In the classroom, the procedures should be as follows:

    - Raise your hand in order to be asked to speak.

    - One person will speak at a time.

    - Remain at your desk unless you have the teacher's permission to be elsewhere.

    - If you are given permission to leave the room for any reason or if your whole class is going somewhere in the building, you are to walk.

    - Most important: *Always treat your classmates as you want to be treated.*

6. When we are in the sanctuary for any activity, we are to remember that the sanctuary is always a quiet place for everyone, a place where we show our respect for other people, as well as for all things in the room. Therefore, we are careful with our voices, hands, and feet.

The purpose of these guidelines is to assure each child quality education, personal growth, and a very pleasant experience in our religious school. Students who follow the guidelines will discover that learning is enhanced and that great strides in finding a personal Jewish identity will be made.

Parents of students in Grades 2-8 will be notified weekly of student compliance with these guidelines. If student behavior becomes a frequent problem for the teacher and other students in the class, parents will be asked to a conference with the teacher and the rabbi. Parents may be asked to sit in the classroom until the problem behavior is corrected. In an extreme case, continued attendance by a student at religious school may be denied.

These rules are simple and basic. They should permit each child to get the most from the religious school educational experience.

I have discussed these guidelines with my child(ren):

Parent's Signature _____

I have discussed these guidelines with my parents:

Student's Signature _____

Discipline Policy

Bet Shalom Religious School
Kenosha-Racine, Wisconsin

1. No physical punishment or physical force shall be used during school hours or on school grounds, except when needed to protect other students or the teacher (e.g., in the case of a physical fight between students).

2. Every effort shall be made to deal with discipline in a respectful, quiet, informational, and personal manner. One-on-one talks in private are preferred to public criticism whenever possible.

3. When repetitive disruptive behavior occurs, a call to or a conference with the parent is called for.

4. In extreme situations where a child needs to be removed from the classroom, he/she is to be escorted to the administrative office by the teacher. At this point, a parent shall be contacted immediately.

5. There shall be no profanity utilized in the classroom.

6. Any staff violation of this discipline policy: For a first offense, the administrative team shall investigate the situation. If the behavior is determined to be inappropriate, the team shall recommend to the Bet Shalom Religious School Board that the employee be placed on probation. The final decision shall be made by the Bet Shalom Religious School Board by a vote. Any further incidence can result in automatic dismissal after an investigation and recommendation by the administrative team to the Bet Shalom Religious School Board. The final decision shall be voted on by the Bet Shalom Religious School Board.

7. In extreme circumstances, the administrative team can recommend to the Bet Shalom Religious School Board the immediate dismissal of an employee. The Bet Shalom Religious School Board shall then vote on it.

8. We recognize that situations not covered by this policy may arise. Any concerns that seem to fall outside these categories shall be brought to the administrative team for individual review.

9. It is expected that all staff employed by the Bet Shalom Religious School will operate within these guidelines.

Discipline Policies

Congregation Tifereth Jacob

Discipline Philosophy

The School Board of Congregation Tifereth Jacob feels that each individual should have the following rights:

1. The right to learn without interference from other people in the school or class

2. The right to work together as student and teachers in an atmosphere of mutual respect and understanding

3. The right to have one's personal property respected by others

4. The right to be protected from physical harm

Expectations of Behavior

1. Students will be ready to participate in class activities.

2. Students will not disrupt any other student's participation in class activities.

3. Students will not touch other students in a manner that could be considered offensive or disruptive or use language that could be considered offensive or disruptive.

4. Students will not abuse the property of Congregation Tifereth Jacob or its facility.

5. Students will behave in accordance with the spirituality of our sanctuary at all times. The sanctuary is not to be used as a passageway to other rooms of our facility. Such items as skateboards, in-line skates, or sport cleats will not be permitted in that room at any time for any reason.

6. Students will remain *on campus at all times*, from the time they are dropped off until the time they are picked up. This means they cannot leave the CTJ part of the Ladera School grounds at any time. Help us by making sure your student goes directly into CTJ's school office or his/her classroom. If a student is discovered leaving the campus, parents will be notified *immediately*.

To ensure these expectations are achieved, the following will be enforced:

- Classroom standards will be established by each teacher and students on the first day of school and a written list of these standards will be mailed home. This *berit hakitah,* "classroom covenant," is to be signed by the student and parents and returned to the teacher at the next school session.

- The following are all prohibited: defiance, stealing, vandalism, dishonesty, profanity and vulgarity, fighting, drugs, alcohol, tobacco.

Discipline Procedure

1. If there are consistent violations of the *berit hakitah* (classroom standards), the *teacher* will confer with the *student,* and *written notice* will be mailed home.

2. If infractions continue, the *education director* will confer with the *teacher* and the *student,* and *written notice* will be mailed home.

3. If there are further problems, *parents* will be called for a conference with the *teacher,* the *education director,* and/or the *rabbi* and *student* to determine further action, which may include any or all of the following:

   - Parents on premises during school hours

   - Isolation of the student within the school setting away from the class

   - Suspension for a period of time with satisfactory completion of homework/study assignments

   - Any mutually agreed-upon arrangements made at a conference of the parent, the student, and CTJ personnel

If your student is suspended from the religious school:

- The School Board will monitor actions of all suspended students to determine if readmission is possible after a prescribed time.

- Severe Clause: In case of extreme or unusual circumstances, the preceding sequence may be suspended and action may be taken at the discretion of the education director, the rabbi, and/or the School Board.

APPENDIX G

FAMILY EDUCATION

In the introduction to her book *Learning Together: A Sourcebook on Jewish Family Education* (A.R.E., 1987), Janice P. Alper, RJE, writes that our families need schools to nurture Jewish knowledge and provide moral and psychological support. However, our schools must be able to call upon the home to implement, reinforce, and enhance the teachings, practices, and values of our heritage. How do we work with the home to foster the spirit of Judaism? How do we help people not born to Judaism—not raised with Jewish memories, not connected to Israel, Jewish prayer, or the Hebrew language—identify with the history, values, and practices of Judaism? And how do we help those born into a Jewish home develop, maintain, and transmit to their children a Jewish life-style and mind-set?

A school needs to develop programs that involve parents in the study of Jewish content parallel to their children's study, programs in Jewish literacy that deal with skills connected to Jewish holidays, and programs that introduce participants to Jewish texts and resources.

In the Winter 1990 issue of *Compass*, Ms. Alper delineates four criteria for the implementation of family education programs:

1. The programs should involve the entire family. Learning activities should be structured to appeal to all the generations in the family. Some of the learning activities may be done interactively, with all family members participating together; other activities may be parallel, with children separated from adults but using the same content.

2. The programs should be rich in Jewish content and provide primary source material (selections from our classic religious literature), as well as other documents that expose people to a wide range of Jewish choices.

3. The programs should affect change that is transferable beyond the immediate setting and should develop one or more methods that allow participants to bring what they have learned into their homes and everyday lives.

4. The programs should encompass a range of families, including

those with different family structures and observance patterns, and link families to other families so no family feels isolated or alone.

Family Day

This is an occasional session, possibly one a year for each grade, when parents and children attend class together for the entire religious school day. The session may include "special" elements, but it should be based on the class curriculum, involving discussions and projects where parents and children learn and work together.

Parallel Classes

Parents of the children in the religious school may spend time during school hours studying the same material their children are studying in class. Such a program can be divided into smaller segments that reflect the curriculum of a specific grade or a particular topic studied by several grades.

A Note to Parents, Our Educational Partners

To accomplish the goals of our religious school, we need you to be our vocal partners. The children are a Jewish community's most precious possession. While we strive to do the best we can in the short time we have with them each week, we often wish we could achieve more.

You, as parents, are in a wonderful position because you have so many more hours with your children each week than we do. Therefore, we are asking you to become our partners in the creation of the best possible Jewish experience for the youth of our community. Remember that our children look to us as role models. If you show your children that Judaism and Jewish learning are important to you, these things will become important to them. Below are a few suggestions for the continuation of Jewish education outside the classroom:

1. Prepare your child for the opening of religious school. Impress upon the child the importance of learning and how Jewish education will make them more knowledgeable Jews and better people.

2. Take an interest in the materials and notices that your child brings home throughout the school year. Discuss regularly the work of the class in terms of your child's everyday activities. Your interest will serve as a stimulus to your child, creating increased effort and excitement.

3. Take an active interest in all school projects, not only the ones in which your own child is involved. Join us for holiday celebrations and special activities. Inform the school about any particular talents or interests you would be willing to share with the students. Parent participation will be greatly appreciated. Share any information you have about trips or attractions that have Jewish relevance and about any Jewish organizations that provide speakers, films, or other resources.

4. Try to interest your child in Jewish books. Encourage listening to Jewish music and the viewing of special programs and films. Bring Judaism into your home by displaying works of art and ritual objects. Remember that a *chanukiah* can be displayed throughout the year, Shabbat candles can be lit every Friday night, matzah ball soup is delicious any time, and children love to help select a *mezuzah* for the front door of the house. Show your children that using their eyes, noses, ears, fingers, and tongues will help them experience the joy of Judaism in their home.

Parents as Partners

A significant component of our educational program is to to reach out to parents. Teaching *only* the child without the support of the parents and home environment will have little positive effect. Therefore, one of our tasks is to increase school-to-family communication for the purpose of creating the most dynamic partnership possible: child>parent>school.

This approach has several concrete goals:

1. To teach information about Judaism to the whole family

2. To create opportunities for parents to discuss Jewish issues with their children

3. To share written reports of student progress, affording parents and students the opportunity to "write back" to the teacher

4. To allow the child to share the tangible results of his/her learning, which can become long-lasting items in the family's collection of Jewish objects

5. To involve parents with their children in the ongoing learning process

For the Teacher:

1. Letter of Introduction: Each teacher is *required* to write a letter of introduction as the *first in a series* of letters that will be sent home to parents. The letter should convey warmth and excitement about the year ahead, the seriousness you bring to the school and Jewish education, and the importance of creating a partnership between home and school. This letter should also contain a self-introduction, a welcome to the school, the class curriculum/syllabus, major projects for the year, and a class management plan. It may also include an amusing story or an item that will spark curiosity. Parents will be sure to respond.

    Make certain you inform the parents that this letter is only a "first" in a series of letters to be sent to them.

2. Sunshine Telegram: It is important to use a device to inform parents on a regular basis that their child is doing very well. This is true especially for younger children.

This *Sunshine Telegram* is being sent to bring you the happy news that _____ has _____ in class this week. I am sure this wonderful work will continue!

Congratulations!

Your Teacher

By using this kind of reinforcement *regularly*, you will make the parents and students aware that if they do not receive this written acknowledgement, the child's work is less than excellent.

3. Homework Assignments: These should be accompanied by a cover letter, should involve both children and parents, and should be non-threatening to parents who do not have an adequate Judaic background. Family projects should take no more than twenty minutes to complete successfully. If a family wants to take more time, good for them!

   - *Primary Grades*—Family involvement can be as simple as sending home an art project and explaining its use in a home ritual (e.g., coasters decorated with the ten plagues to be used at a Passover seder, apples-in-honey place mats for Rosh Hashanah, games for Jewish holidays, etc.).

   - *Upper Grades*—Family games are also applicable for the upper grades. Interviews with family members also work well, especially if the questions focus on personal memories, providing a vehicle for intergenerational sharing. Sharing family recipes is a good extension of the interview. Discussion questions-of-the-week (or month) offer family members an opportunity to communicate with one another, as do *mitzvah* projects—either holiday-associated or of a general nature.

   Simple sharings work very well: photos of class activities, an audio-cassette or videotape of a class project or even of a typical class day. *Involvement does not mean that an assignment has to be returned to school.*

4. Create-a-Custom: Provide families with some background and guidance to create a custom that they themselves can adapt for a specific holiday or associate with a *mitzvah* students are learning about in school.

5. Year-end Shebangs: Many classes already participate in some closing activity that involves food. Below are some ideas that go beyond the edible:

- *Game Shows*—Any of the formats of the most popular shows lend themselves to class review and culmination. "Password," "Hollywood Squares," "Tic-Tac-Dough," and "Scrabble" are a few of the simple ones.

  Families can play as a team, or teams can be created by using various adult/child groupings.

- *Media Shows*—Videos and slide shows are great culminating projects, which can be handled two ways: Parents and students together can write/produce/direct/act in them, or students can do all the work. In either case, a joint viewing on the last day of school is a fine closure for the year.

- *Performances, Plays, Debates, Trials, Etc.*—As with the media shows, parents can be participants or observers. I know of a class with a great track record for such a project, an annual "Conference on a United Judaism." Students are the main participants in a debate format, but questions from the floor are encouraged, and parents are always invited.

These suggestions are just the tip of the iceberg. Share your favorite and/or most workable idea with the educator, who will share it through the teacher's bulletin. We will all continue to learn with one another.

Remember: Keep those parents involved!

APPENDIX H

TEACHER STUFF

Teaching Tips

Plan a good closure that can be used for any subject matter. After completing a unit of study, prepare a number of paper strips with *incomplete sentences* that pertain to the subject matter. The incomplete sentences must be thought-provoking and should offer more than one possibility for completion, e.g., "The Holocaust happened because...." Prepare enough strips of incomplete sentences so that you have one strip for every two students.

Have the students work in pairs, drawing a strip from a box. Have each student in the pair complete the sentence on that strip and share his/her response with the other students, who will choose which sentence completion they think is better.

Maintain a *positive classroom.* A rule I always included on my list of classroom procedures was "No Put-Downs." Unfortunately, children often enjoy put-downs. Not in my classroom! Students are so accustomed to saying things the wrong way that they do not think about how people feel when put down. Spend a few minutes explaining how negative it is to think this way. It will be time well spent, and the positive atmosphere of your classroom will be increased.

On 3 x 5 index cards, write comments that appear to be compliments but if said sarcastically become put-downs, e.g., "You're really smart," "Who cuts your hair?" or "Where did you get that outfit?"

Before using the cards, brainstorm with the students, compiling a list of additional statements that can be used as both compliments and put-downs. Write each statement on a separate card. Have two students share a card. Ask one student to read the card as a compliment. Ask: How does it feel to receive a compliment? Then have the other student read the same card as a put-down. Ask: How does it feel to be put down? Repeat this procedure several times with different students. You can close the activity by having students sit in a sharing circle and asking each student to say something nice about another student. Be sure each child is mentioned at least once.

Fifteen Ways to Improve Classroom Teaching/Learning

(Adapted from an article by Helmar Wagner, a professor of curriculum and instruction, in the October 1984 issue of *The Pedagogic Reporter*.)

Establish a positive classroom atmosphere. Using all possible means (e.g., surveys, positive self-esteem activities, dialogues, etc.), get to know your students. Be encouraging and supportive.

Know your students (before class begins). Learn whatever you can about your students, their family, pets, likes and dislikes, hobbies, special interests, etc. Do *not* prejudge them by past performances in other classes.

"Teaching is a human relations profession, and learning is enhanced when the teacher and student can relate to each other."

Involve the students. "Learning by doing" is the best way. Busy classes that are product-oriented are less likely to be disruptive. Let students have some input into the planning of activities so they have some "ownership" of what is taking place. Don't be afraid to assign leadership roles to shy and even disruptive students to give them some recognition. Let students work in small groups of two or three to accomplish a task.

Exercise positive classroom control. "I hear someone talking" works better than scolding an individual in front of the whole class. Those few students who misbehave need to know that the learning atmosphere is being disrupted, but the entire class doesn't need to stop working while you address one individual. For positive classroom control, get up and move around the classroom.

Know the materials being presented. You cannot wait until the last minute to prepare a lesson. It is important not only to be well prepared but to know the materials well. Good preparation leads to better instruction. (Furthermore, students know when you are not well prepared.)

Hold the students' attention. You can hold some students' attention for only twelve to fifteen minutes. When their interest begins to dwindle (and you will know when that happens), you need to change gears and use another approach. Always plan more activities than you think you will need. If one activity doesn't work, be prepared to shift course in midstream.

Use proper questioning techniques. If done properly, the questioning process will get the students involved in the learning process. The teacher must be open to student responses and listen to them. Questions that encourage student thinking instead of memorized responses will produce a more positive learning experience. Questions that require analysis are often more likely to create classroom discussion than questions that can elicit only a "yes" or "no" answer. Asking for clarification of answers will also stimulate additional thought about a question. Asking for reasons for their answers forces the students to justify them. Asking the right questions is a very important part of a lesson.

Provide appropriate rewards. This doesn't mean that you should buy little gifts. The key word in this case is "appropriate." The reward can be as simple as public recognition or verbal praise. Above all, be positive and supportive to encourage the students.

Work with individuals. Give some individual attention to students who are uninvolved or do not participate. Time spent with these students might provide the impetus to help them over a hurdle, and they will know that you care. (I'll never forget a young man who joined the youth group and sat quietly in the back of the room without participating. When I discovered that he was teaching himself to play the guitar, I gave him a NFTY Songster and told him to learn the songs. He not only learned them, he eventually became the regional song leader and is now a rabbi. See what you can do!)

Use your voice properly. Keep your voice soothing. A pleasant voice is important. Be aware that the students can hear the "music" of your voice: anger, love, sarcasm, etc.

Be patient. Learning is sometimes a slow process. Continued repetition is often necessary before a student receives the message. Identify different ways of repeating the message. If the students don't learn it one way, they will learn it another way. Just be patient.

Take pride in your appearance. If the students must dress appropriately, why not the teacher?

Have a sense of humor. A smile goes a long way in a classroom!

Use "we" instead of "I" or "me." "We will look at a Jewish calendar" is much more inclusive than "I will show you a Jewish calendar." In your classroom you are trying to form a community, and "we" sounds much more like a group.

HAVE FUN!

Asking Appropriate Questions

According to Bloom's Taxonomy, there are six levels of thinking. They are listed below, beginning with the lowest level:

Knowledge:
Learning from information

Ask questions that include one of the following: identify, define, list, label, recall, state, name, who, what, when, where.

Comprehension:
Understanding the information

Ask questions using one of the following: interpret, discuss, describe, explain, report, illustrate.

Application:
Using the information

Ask questions using one of the following: show, use, apply, practice, illustrate, demonstrate, classify.

Analysis:
Examining specific parts of the information

Ask questions using one of the following: decode, classify, order, distinguish, compare, analyze.

Synthesis:
Doing something new and different with the information

Ask questions using one of the following: create, improve, compose, design, change, reconstruct.

Evaluation:
Judging the information

Ask questions using one of the following: judge, select, rank, evaluate, critique.

Based on Leviticus 19, the following are examples of some questions you can ask at the different levels:

Knowledge:
Identify the statement from which Leviticus 19, known as the "Holiness Code," derives its name.

Comprehension:
What do you think the writer meant when he wrote: "You shall be holy, for I, *Adonai* your God, am holy?"

Application:	What are the characteristics of a holy person?
Analysis:	What does to be holy mean?
Synthesis:	Create rules for a society that is holy. What would be expected of the people who live in such a society? Create an ad/publicity campaign to "sell" your society.
Evaluation:	Would it be possible to establish such a society in today's world, and how would it be done? If it is not possible, what can each person do to approach holiness?

The following additional words may lead some students to think:

Identify, recognize, remember, compare, reorder, solve, which, what is, choose, reason, deduce, detect, support, predict, produce, write, design, develop, decide, assess.

Questioning

The art of questioning is worth considering in detail. Most of your work in the classroom will involve questioning, and learning will be affected by your skill in this area.

To question well is to teach well. Questions should make children think and act. A good question is direct and to the point; concise, simple, and clear in meaning; on the students' language level; and logical in content.

The technique of good questioning may be best demonstrated by giving examples of the most common errors:

> The double question: Where is Palestine, and what are its boundaries?
>
> The ambiguous question: What happens when it rains?
>
> The indefinite question: What about the prophet Isaiah?
>
> The guessing question: Was Amos right or wrong in this instance?
>
> The echo question: Moses brought down the Tablets of the Law. Who brought down the Tablets of the Law?
>
> The pumping question: Whose last name was Maim?

The above questions also do not challenge the students. Unfortunately, the teacher often gives the student an easy way out of a questioning situation, e. g., "Do you think saying 'I'm sorry' is always a sufficient answer to an error?" The student who does not want to think or who has not been paying attention may just answer "no." A better question would be: "Why is saying 'I'm sorry' not always a sufficient answer to an error?" The child *must* think in order to provide *any* answer.

Similarly, the manner in which you call on children when questioning them is important. If you point to a child or call a child's name before asking your question, the rest of the class will not have to think of an answer. They will look at the child who is struggling to answer and think how lucky they are that they were not chosen. Ask your question first before calling on a child to answer.

Finally, do not use an obvious, preconceived technique for calling on children. Some teachers make the mistake of calling on the children alphabetically or according to the seating arrangement. Again, the children know who is next in order, and they *think* only when it is *their* turn.

A vibrant, alert teacher results in an alert class. Include the entire class by calling on every child at least once during each lesson. But keep the class alert by calling on some students more often, lest the children feel that one question per lesson is their limit.

V'shinantam

October/November 1994
UAHC Southwest Teacher News

Creating Jewish Holiday Stories

(*For Primary Grades*)

Make copies of pictures that have to do with the holiday discussed in your unit of study (e.g., Jewish symbols, holiday symbols, ritual objects, food, people celebrating the holiday, etc.).

Elicit titles for stories based on your holiday choice. If your subject is Shabbat, some titles could be: The Day I Lost the Sabbath Candles; How I Celebrate Shabbat; Making Challah; Setting the Table; etc. List the children's ideas for story titles on the chalkboard and guide them in studying the list. Have each student choose a title and print that title on the top of two blank sheets of paper. Have the children spread out the pictures on the table and select those pictures that are related to their story title. Have them glue the pictures onto one of the sheets under their story title. On the other sheet, have them write a story that goes with the title, including the names of each picture they have selected for their story. After the children share their stories with the class, compile the stories into a booklet.

(*For Intermediate Grades*)

Israel Geography

On the wall, post a large map of the State of Israel and its surrounding neighbors. On index cards, prepare the names and pictures of historical Israeli landmarks, cities, geographical locations, etc. Pass out the cards to pairs of students and have them identify the location of the places/things on their cards.

Israel Map Quiz Game

On the wall, post a large map of Israel with its neighboring countries. On index cards, prepare a number of quiz statements. Below are some examples:

Israel signed a peace agreement with this country to its south.

This city begins with the letter H and is the largest port in Israel.

David Ben-Gurion made his home here.

This city begins with the letter S and was the home of the Jewish mystics.

Prepare at least twelve statements and have the children prepare at least twelve more. When you have twenty-four or more quiz statements, you are ready to start the game.

Divide the class into small groups. Have one member of each group choose a card; instruct another member to read the statement; then tell the group to confer on the answer. Ask one group member to give the answer and the rest of the group to point out the location on the map. For each correct answer, the group will receive twenty points. Continue playing until all the quiz statements have been used. The winning team gets to do something special.

A Mitzvah Bulletin Board

Make your students aware that there are needy people and how we, as Jews, can help them. Cover a bulletin board with brightly colored paper. Write a title on the top of the bulletin board, e.g., Mitzvah Heroes or Mitzvah Doers.

Ask the students to bring in news articles about disasters, children in need, families in crises, etc., and post these articles on the bulletin board.

Encourage your students to help others, either those in need featured in the articles or someone they know. After the children have done something to help another person, tell them to draw an outline of their hand and write a short description of what they did. Post the "helping hands" on the bulletin board.

Interviews with the Elderly

Jewish history comes alive when it is told by a person who has lived it. Help the students develop a list of questions they can use to interview an elderly person. That person can be a grandparent or a member of the congregation. Plan a visit to a home for the aged, where each child may also choose one person to interview. Below are some sample questions for these interviews:

- When and where were you born?
- What was your favorite activity as a child?
- How old were you at that time?
- How did you celebrate _____ ? (Insert the name of a holiday or Shabbat.)
- Describe your family: brothers, sisters, extended family.
- What was your home like?
- What did you do for entertainment?
- What kind of food did you eat?
- What was your favorite food?
- What was school like?
- Describe your favorite teacher.
- What kind of chores did you have to do at home?
- What kind of work did your parents do?
- How did you get around from one place to another (transportation)?
- How were you treated as a Jew?
- Who were your friends?

Have the students conduct individual interviews, taking notes or taping the responses. When the interviews are complete, divide the class into small groups according to who was interviewed: grandparents, members of the congregation, or people from the home for the aged. The reports should include facts about the lives of these people, what the students learned from them, and what the students learned about Jewish life during these people's youth. Have the students share what they learned.

Fly Away

Do you remember how as children we used to make an airplane from a piece of paper? Make a paper airplane, write a lesson or activity on it, and "fly it." Whatever you write should make a point that pertains to your lesson. Have the student who catches the plane read the lesson or do the activity. Can you imagine the look on the children's faces when you make the airplane "fly away"?

Reading Pictures

Provide some pictures that pertain to your subject matter (e.g., holidays, Bible stories, and such Jewish concepts as sharing, helping others, feeding the hungry, etc.).

Have each child choose a picture for discussion. Have the child tell what he/she sees or "reads" in the picture. Ask: What story is the picture telling? Help the students, as necessary, to learn the lesson for the day.

Provide sentence strips for each child. Help him/her write a sentence about a picture. Have the students read their sentence. Then hang their pictures and sentences in the classroom.

Getting to Know You: An Opening Day Activity

Prepare an index card for each student in the class. On each card, write one direction such as:

> Find out Steve's favorite Jewish holiday.
>
> Find out Michelle's favorite color.
>
> Find out Joe's favorite Jewish song.

Put the cards into a small bag. Have the children wear name tags and sit in a circle. While music is playing, tell the students to pass the bag around the circle. Stop the music! Have the child who is holding the bag pick a card from the bag and follow the directions on the card. Continue playing until every child has had a turn.

A Bill of Rights for a Child
with an Attention Deficit Disorder

"HELP ME TO FOCUS"

Please teach me through my sense of "touch." I need "hands-on"
and body movement.

"I NEED TO KNOW WHAT COMES NEXT"

Please give me a structured environment where there is a dependable routine. Give me an advanced warning if there will be changes.

"WAIT FOR ME; I'M STILL THINKING"

Please allow me to go at my own pace. If I rush, I get confused and upset.

"I'M STUCK; I CAN'T DO IT!"

Please offer me options for problem solving.
I need to know the detours when the road is blocked.

"IS IT RIGHT? I NEED TO KNOW NOW!"

Please give me rich and immediate feedback on how I'm doing.

"I DIDN'T FORGET; I DIDN'T 'HEAR' IT IN THE FIRST PLACE"

Please give me directions one step at a time, and ask me to repeat
what I think you said.

"I DIDN'T KNOW I WASN'T IN MY SEAT!"

Please remind me to stop, think, and act.

"AM I ALMOST DONE NOW?"

Please give me short work periods with short-term goals.

"WHAT?"

Please don't say, "I've already told you that."
Tell me again in different words.
Give me a signal. Draw me a symbol.

"I KNOW IT'S ALL WRONG; ISN'T IT?"

Please give me praise for partial success. Reward me for self-improvement,
not just for perfection.

"BUT WHY DO I ALWAYS GET YELLED AT?"

Please catch me doing something right,
and praise me for my specific positive behavior.
Remind me (and yourself) about my good points
when I'm having a bad day.

Introducing God
into the Classroom

This true-false worksheet was originally developed by Rabbi Roland B. Gittelsohn for the *Student Workbook to A Little Lower Than the Angels,* published by the UAHC in 1955. We share this helpful tool with teachers who are looking for ways to introduce a discussion of God into the classroom. This worksheet can be used in several ways: in its entirety, to start a discussion or a unit; piecemeal throughout the school year; or as a summation for the year or for a unit.

1. God answers all our prayers if we pray properly.   T F

2. God is like a great wise man who knows the answers to all the questions in the world.   T F

3. God knows everything that happens to us.   T F

4. God is the force or power behind everything that halogens on this cartel.   T F

5. Religion and science disagree on most important questions about life and its meaning.   T F

6. Evolution is the proper concern of science; it has nothing to do with religion.   T F

7. The scientific explanation of how the world began and the tory of Creation in the Bible do not necessarily conflict.   T F

8. A person can believe in God, yet not be religious.   T F

9. The miracles reported in the Bible probably occurred very much as they are described there.   T F

10. A person who believes in God and lives a righteous life may suffer just as much sadness and misfortune as others do.   T F

11. My conscience is part of God.   T F

12. Of all the forms of life on this earth, only human beings have souls.   T F

13. Everyone who lives an ethical life is religious.   T F

14. Some part of every human being lives on after his/her death.   T F

15. After death, good people go to heaven, and wicked people go to hell.   T F

16. God protects from all harm those who really trust God.   T F

17. God is like a king who wants us to worship and please God.   T F

18. God is in heaven.   T F

19. A knowledge of science can lead to a better understanding of God.   T F

20. Suffering is punishment for our sins.   T F

21. Good people generally live longer than bad people.   T F

22. We can help answer our own prayers.   T F

23. God cannot perform miracles.   T F

24. God is in part a combination of all the ethical ideals a human being should try to follow.   T F

25. The purpose of prayer is to help us get the things we want in life.   T F

26. One of the most important purposes of prayer is to help us improve our conduct.   T F

27. With so much war, crime, and suffering in the world, it is hard to believe in God.   T F

28. Religious questions and problems are important to me; I think about them quite a bit.   T F

29. God is our Heavenly Father.   T F

30. I definitely believe in God.   T F

31. My idea of God is extremely vague and indefinite.   T F

32. There are many questions about the meaning of life that religion cannot answer.   T F

33. I see little real value or use in praying.   T F

34. Attending religious services has little or nothing to do with being religious.   T F

35. People who fear God are more religious than those who do not.   T F

36. Prayer can help us solve some of our most serious problems.   T F

37. Prayer can help a sick person recover.   T F

38. Religion has no right to interfere with the way a man conducts his business or industry. T F

39. The Ten Commandments are at least as important and necessary today as when they were first given to our ancestors. T F

40. Religion can help us cope with trouble and sorrow. T F

God Talk

(Based on *Finding God* by Rifat Sonsino and Daniel B. Syme.)

Six Assumptions about God

1. Everyone thinks about God.

2. No one *knows* what God is or isn't.

3. There is no one authoritative, universally accepted Jewish concept of God.

4. Respected Jewish thinkers have different ways of writing, thinking, and speaking about God.

5. The only points on which all Jews who *do* believe in God agree is that God is one and God is invisible.

6. Our ideas of God change as we grow and mature.

Jewish Thinkers/Thinking about God

Biblical Concept: God is anthropomorphic (having human form). God is anthropropathic (having human emotions). God's functions are Creation, Revelation, and Redemption.

Rabbinic Period: God is still considered anthropomorphic and anthropopathic, but more distant. Refer to the end of the Book of Deuteronomy for Moses' relationship with God. The rabbis considered being close to God (as Moses was) to be blasphemy. The rabbis inserted "code words" for God into the siddur: *Hamakom,* "The Place"; *Hashem,* "The Name"; *Ribono shel Olam*, "Ruler of the World"; and *Avinu Malkenu*, "Our Father, our King."

The concept of God held by most Jews stops here because these are the ideas to which they've been exposed. Unfortunately, when these ideas or images don't work for them, Jews often abandon Judaism.

Philo and "Spiritual Monotheism": God is pure spirit. God created reason and intelligence. Reason and intelligence created the world.

Rambam (12th century): In simple terms, the only real attribute of the essence of God is a negative one.

> We can't define what God *is*.
> We can only define what God *is not*.

The more intellectual interpretation, based on Aristotelianism, is that God is pure thought/intellect. God thinks the ideas that become the universe. Our intellect grasps what God is thinking by seeing God's world. We can develop our minds sufficiently to approach the possibility of thinking some of the thoughts God is thinking.

Since Moses was the greatest thinker, only he could give us the Torah.

Luria/Mystics/Zohar/Tzimtzum: In simple terms, God cannot be defined. God is *En Sof*, "The Endless One." The more intellectual interpretation deals with the *sefirot*, interlocking concentric circles of power.

Isaac Luria, considered to be the founder of the school of mysticism, believed God voluntarily contracted (*tzimtzum*) to leave space for the physical world. During this process of contracting, certain divine vessels broke, scattering divine sparks throughout the world. Gathering up these divine sparks through *mitzvot* and prayer, human beings in partnership with God can perfect the world.

Rationalists and "Ethical Monotheism" (19th century): To be real human beings, we need:

    A. Cause and effect...science...determinism

    B. Freedom to operate in the predetermined world...ethics

Therefore, God is the Transcendent Unifying Idea that makes the above paradox possible.

Spinoza and Pantheism: God is nature. God is identical with the universe. There is no supernatural.

Martin Buber: Perfect knowledge can be obtained only through a dialogue. There are two ways to establish this dialogue:

"I - It"   Objects, numbers, and sometimes people

"I - Thou" Open, vulnerable relationship with the experiences of the other (for people, animals, and objects of nature)

God is the *"Eternal Thou,"* waiting for us to be courageous enough to enter the *"I-Thou"* relationship, waiting for us to open ourselves to the presence of God.

Milton Steinberg and Limited Theism: God's powers are limited. God is like a parent. Parents love their children and would do anything for them, but parents can't save their children from every evil. God has a fierce love for each of us but cannot protect us from everything. When we feel pain, God weeps.

Mordecai Kaplan (20th century): We need reassurance that the world works. God represents the processes of nature that cooperate with our need for a sense of security.

Jewish Theological Role Models

Give a Jewish label to what the students already believe. Help them understand that spiritually they are a part of the Jewish people and can continue to grow within that community.

Methodology

1. Remind the students that there is no one Jewish concept of God and that they may come to believe ideas other than those they have now.

2. The teacher's own beliefs may be expressed but should be clearly labeled as personal.

3. Talk to the children about God at their appropriate developmental level.

4. When children volunteer their personal concept of God, connect that concept to a mainstream Jewish thinker.

5. Correct obvious factual errors.

6. Do not be embarrassed to say "I don't know."

7. Consult with other teachers/educators/rabbis.

8. Encourage the children to share what they think, feel, and know about God, as well as their own moments of experiencing God.

9. Listen to what the children are saying.

10. Enable the children to consider their participation in Jewish life as a manifestation of their belief in God.

Ways to Praise Students

In an article in the September 1972 issue of *Teacher*, Edward S. Kubany suggested various ways to say "good for you."

1. That's real nice.
2. That's great.
3. I like the way you are.
4. Much better.
5. Keep it up.
6. It's a pleasure to teach when you work like this.
7. What neat work.
8. This kind of work pleases me very much.
9. Terrific.
10. Beautiful.
11. Excellent work.
12. I appreciate your help.
13. Why don't you show the class?
14. Marvelous.
15. That looks as if it's going to be a great report.
16. My goodness, how impressive.
17. You're on the right track now.
18. That's "A" work.
19. It looks as if you put a lot of work into this.
20. That's clever.
21. Very creative.
22. Good thinking.
23. Now you've got the hang of it.
24. Exactly right.
25. Superior work.
26. That's a good point.
27. That's a good observation.
28. You've got it now.
29. Nice going.
30. You make it look easy.

About the Authors

We have both spent our entire professional lives involved with religious education.

Rabbi Lawrence N. Mahrer is in his fourth decade as a congregational rabbi and educator, working almost exclusively in small congregations.

Debi Mahrer Rowe, a graduate of Hebrew Union College-Jewish Institute of Religion Rhea High School of Education in Los Angeles, has worked in a variety of congregations, as well as for a major Jewish publisher.

Both authors are members of NATE, and Debi is an elected member of the NATE board.